William Etridge McLennan

In His Footsteps

A Record of travel to and in the Land of Christ

William Etridge McLennan

In His Footsteps
A Record of travel to and in the Land of Christ

ISBN/EAN: 9783337067472

Printed in Europe, USA, Canada, Australia, Japan

Cover: Foto ©Lupo / pixelio.de

More available books at **www.hansebooks.com**

THE FOOTSTEPS SERIES

IN HIS FOOTSTEPS

A RECORD OF TRAVEL TO AND IN THE LAND OF CHRIST
WITH AN ATTEMPT TO MARK THE LORD'S
JOURNEYINGS IN CHRONOLOGICAL
ORDER FROM HIS BIRTH
TO HIS ASCENSION

By WILLIAM E. McLENNAN

NEW YORK: EATON & MAINS
CINCINNATI: CURTS & JENNINGS
1896

Copyright by
EATON & MAINS.
1896.

Composition, electrotyping,
printing, and binding by
EATON & MAINS,
150 Fifth Ave., New York.

CONTENTS.

	PAGE
INTRODUCTORY NOTE	7
PREFACE	9

CHAPTER I.
OVER SEA TO BETHLEHEM.................................... 17

CHAPTER II.
FROM THE BIRTH OF CHRIST TO THE BEGINNING OF HIS MINISTRY, B. C. 5–A. D. 27.................................... 3

CHAPTER III.
FIRST YEAR'S MINISTRY, JANUARY TO DECEMBER, A. D. 27...... 47

CHAPTER IV.
SECOND YEAR'S MINISTRY, JANUARY TO DECEMBER, A. D. 28.... 61

CHAPTER V.
THIRD YEAR'S MINISTRY, JANUARY TO DECEMBER, A. D. 29...... 71

CHAPTER VI.
FOURTH YEAR'S MINISTRY, JANUARY TO APRIL 2, A. D. 30...... 85

CHAPTER VII.
PASSION WEEK.................................... 92

CHAPTER VIII
THE FORTY DAYS, FROM THE RESURRECTION TO THE ASCENSION, A. D. 30.................................... 105

ILLUSTRATIONS.

	PAGE		PAGE
The Rock in the Mosque of Omar, Jerusalem	FRONTISPIECE	Jacob's Well	55
Map: New York to Bethlehem	16	Eastern House, Showing Flat Roof and Courtyard	59
S. S. Lahn, of the North German Lloyd Line	18	Map	60
Gibraltar	20	The Horns of Hattin	63
Jaffa, from the North	22	Funeral Scene in Palestine	65
A Jerusalem Jew	25	Tombs on the Road to Nain	66
An Arab	26	The Sea of Galilee	67
Highway, with Cactus Hedge	27	Map	70
An Oriental Street	28	Modern Tyre	74
Bethlehem, From the Valley of the Shepherds	29	A Blind Beggar	77
Map	30	The Waters of Merom	78
Bethlehem, Showing Church of the Nativity	32	Cæsarea Philippi	79
The Chapel of the Nativity	33	A Little Child of Palestine	80
Jerusalem—The Mosque of Omar	35	Bethany	82
In the Land of Egypt, Raising Water from the Nile for Irrigation	37	Map	84
Tent Life in Palestine	38	"The Bloody Way"	86
Nazareth	39	Woman with Headdress of Coins	87
Galilean Caravan Approaching Jerusalem	41	Lepers Begging by the Wayside	89
Jesus and the Doctors	42	Plan of Herod's Temple	91
Interior of a Peasant's House	44	Bethany, Olivet, and Jerusalem	93
Map	46	Map	96
The Jordan, Where John Baptized	48	The Garden of Gethsemane	100
The Wilderness of Judea	49	Map	104
Ruins of Capernaum	52	Rock Tomb with Rolling Stone Door	106
Herod's Temple	53	The Church of the Holy Sepulcher, Jerusalem	107
		Pilgrim in the Church of the Holy Sepulcher	108
		The Mount of Olives	110

INTRODUCTORY NOTE.

THE following pages contain the details of a plan by which it is easily possible to interest every boy and girl in the study of history, travel, and biography. I was present at the breakfast party alluded to by the author, and heard the remark of Bishop Vincent. It impressed me likewise, and became the subject of conversation afterward. Out of it came the method of work herein set forth--workable and remarkable, as proved by my own experience.

But, so far as success in winning attention to the life and character of Jesus is concerned, Mr. McLennan must bear the palm. He has held, for two successive years to my personal knowledge, thirty-five Juniors, boys and girls in about equal numbers, from the ages of twelve to sixteen, in this study. They have met once a week from seven to eight o'clock in the evening, with an average attendance of twenty-five. Most of them have become regular attendants at church services, and for knowledge of the sequence of events in the life of our Lord, and the geography of Palestine, they will, on examination, rank higher than an equal number of members in an Annual Conference.

Sunday school teachers with scholars of this age, as well as Junior superintendents, should work this plan. Get the pictures and mount them as directed. Equip yourselves in fancy for the journey and travel with the boys and girls in the

> "holy fields
> Over whose acres walked those blessed feet
> Which eighteen hundred years ago were nailed
> For our advantage on the bitter cross."

No work will so kindle your own interest, nor more richly reward your efforts as a soul-winner. This book and the work connected with it may well constitute a whole year in the course of study for Epworth League Juniors.   EDWIN A. SCHELL.

MRS. HUMPHRY WARD quotes Professor Jowett as saying to her: "We shall come in future to teach almost entirely by biography. We shall begin with the life which is most familiar to us—the life of Christ; and we shall more and more put before our children the examples of great persons' lives, so that they shall have from the beginning heroes and friends in their thoughts."

"All that history which at a distance seemed to float in the clouds of an unreal world took instantly a body, a solidity which astonished me. The striking accord between the texts and the places, the marvelous harmony of the evangelical picture with the country which served as its frame, were to me as a revelation. I had before me a fifth gospel, mutilated but still legible."—*M. Renan.*

PREFACE.

A FEW years ago, just after the writer had entered the ministry, it was his privilege to be entertained with others at a well-known Methodist home whose guest of honor was Bishop Vincent. With that delightful tact for which he is famous the bishop had won from the young theologues present a confession of the perplexities and trials peculiar to their ministerial life. My own problem had reference to the training of boys and girls, especially along intellectual lines. I have never forgotten the bishop's words on that occasion: "A boy or girl who has once become interested in travels will never be satisfied with worthless books." The bishop's long experience, as perhaps the most popular educator in the country, gave to his words peculiar emphasis. I began at once to act upon his suggestion with the most gratifying results. I found, however, that travels alone did not quite fulfill all the conditions for an ideal plan such as I had conceived. There was needed something for which travel is but a means to an end. Mere sightseeing soon becomes tiresome, and when undertaken for its own sake seems rather selfish. My plan seemed complete when I united with travels biography. Besides being deeply interesting, I had long believed biography to be one of the noblest means of inspiration for the young; that, indeed, as Carlyle has put it, "The history of what man has accomplished is at bottom the history of the great men who have worked here." At that time I would scarcely have dared to say what the late Professor Jowett is reported to have said to Mrs. Humphrey Ward, that "We shall come in future to teach almost entirely by biography."

But biography, to be interesting—and boys and girls will not read what is not interesting—must be something more than a dreary detail of names, dates, and ages. Genealogy is not biography. The main, I may say the whole, attraction of any character to a boy or girl, especially to the boy, lies in the con-

Preface.

tinuous movement of events and the rapid transfer of scene. What boy does not love to hear of steamboats, railroads, and the various means of transportation; of strange people and their customs; of plots and counterplots; of defeats and victories? When to the narrative can be added such details that one seems to be actually realizing the scenes of the original life, there is nothing wanting to combine interest and profit. This is not theory but experience. A year or more before the opening of the Columbian Exposition I took a class of older young people, representing various degrees of intelligence, through a course of reading and investigation, beginning with Columbus, marking his footsteps from Italy to Spain, following in his wake to America and, finally, to the city of Valladolid, where he breathed his last. Then, with an introduction on prehistoric America, the steps of the colonists in America were traced, and, by the movements of their descendants, the entire history of our country was brought down to the opening of the great Exposition. Each step of the way was illustrated by means of the stereopticon. A similar plan was, with equal success, pursued with a large class of boys and girls. An imaginary trip to Palestine was proposed and followed out with the most careful attention to the details of choice of routes, time-tables, baggage, etc. On reaching Palestine our aim was actually to realize, as far as possible, the very scenes connected with the life of Jesus from his birth to his crucifixion and ascension. In this the stereopticon was a most valuable aid, but, unfortunately, slides could not be procured of the most important places except at very great expense. That led to an experiment with prints. I searched the offices of Thomas Cook & Son, Gaze & Son, and other international tourist agencies, for illustrations of the route and the country. Some of these I mounted on cardboard and passed around the class for examination while I talked. Finally came the "halftone" reproductions with which the daily newspapers have flooded the country. Many of these are on Palestine, the best of them being a series of splendid views on "The Land of Christ," and that *magnum opus* edited by Bishop Vincent and Dr. J. W. Lee, *The Earthly Footsteps of the Man of Galilee*. With these views almost every footstep of our Lord can be illustrated at trifling cost.

The present work is *an illustration of a method*, such as is described in the foregoing paragraphs. It is suggestive, not

Preface.

exhaustive. It does not profess to be critical, as that term is understood by scholars. Neither does it discuss, but only states, questions with reference to chronology, topography, etc. It is not a commentary, in the awful sense of being homiletic. It seeks only to help the teacher to make real for young people the Christ of history.

It is prepared, at the suggestion of the General Secretary of the Epworth League, the Rev. Edwin A. Schell, D.D., for the special use of Junior League Superintendents, but it is adapted as well for Sunday school teachers and others who are weary of the *haec fabula docet* method of teaching, and prefer to lead their scholars to realize the majesty of a great life. Dr. Schell informs me that similar outlines for St. Paul, Wesley, and others, will follow, constituting "The Footstep Series."

The series begins with the life of our Lord, on the principle that all instruction should begin and end with that "Name which is above every name." Besides, there is no character that suits our method better. He is referred to in the Acts as "Jesus of Nazareth, . . . who *went about* doing good." His life was full of action. He came, bestowed his blessing, and was off to some other place where there were needy ones awaiting him. His journeys took him into all sorts of places, so there is a constant change of scene. We have the busy mart, the temple, the house, the street, the wayside, the sea, the mountain, and the plain following each other in rapid succession. So as we follow in his footsteps this variety cannot fail to attract and hold all young minds and hearts.

It is the living Christ we are to follow. It is not necessary, nor even desirable, that young people should be taught all that they are supposed to believe about Jesus. Rather let them be open to receive impressions in their own way. As they walk in his footsteps from week to week the Lord Christ will appear and reveal his own message. And in the years to come the boys and girls who shall have marked the footsteps of the Lord will in manhood and womanhood recall how their hearts burned within them as they walked and talked with the living Christ, and such memories will, let us be assured, be the strongest ties to bind them to the unseen and eternal.

A WORD TO THE TEACHER.

As already suggested, our plan is to take an imaginary trip to Palestine, and to follow, as far as we are able, the foot-

Preface.

steps of Jesus from his birth in Bethlehem to his ascension. Everything available for making this imaginary journey as realistic as possible should be secured. Get a good map of the world, and, after locating your own town, find out by proper questioning the best way to get to Palestine. Talk over all the available routes, finally selecting one which seems to combine the most advantages. You will, doubtless, decide to sail from New York, though there are other ports from which you might take passage. By correspondence with Messrs. Thomas Cook & Son, or Gaze & Son, New York and Chicago, you will learn all particulars regarding dates of sailing, etc. Discuss routes and steamboat lines. The largest boats run between New York and Liverpool, or Southampton. There are other excellent lines between New York and Glasgow, or Havre. If you should decide on one of these it will be necessary, of course, to cross the Continent by rail. For many reasons I prefer the route *via* Gibraltar and the Mediterranean. The North German Lloyd line of steamers would be chosen for this trip. Whatever route is selected give a description of leaving port, then of your vessel. It will not be difficult to obtain cuts of the interior, the cabin, saloon, engine room, etc. Tell how the boat is propelled or, better, have one of the boys describe the machinery of a steamer. Give a list of the officers, and name the duties of each. Life on board a great steamer will be interesting; how the passengers sleep, what they eat, how they amuse themselves, etc. All such details will make a deep impression, especially on boys. They will begin to read about steamboats and kindred subjects, and as they read their interest in the amours and adventures of disreputable characters will grow less and less. On the itinerary you will observe the different points where your steamer stops. Have views ready of Gibraltar and the other ports, but do not give very much time to these places. Interest should be gradually increased in the country to which we are journeying.

There are many books of travel. Dr. Buckley's *Travels in Three Continents* is, in many respects, one of the very best. It is written in that delightful style for which the author is famous, is up to date, and, above all, accurate. Of books relating to Palestine there are a very large number. *The Land and the Book*, by W. M. Thomson, is exceedingly valuable, but rather expensive. Edersheim's *Life and Times*

Preface.

of *Jesus the Messiah* is a veritable theasury of valuable data bearing on the thoughts and customs of the Jewish people in the time of Christ. *Sinai and Palestine*, by Dean Stanley, is brilliant, but needs revision. The latest work on biblical geography is George Adam Smith's *The Biblical Geography of the Holy Land*. A very valuable little work, and one that embodies the latest discoveries, is *Palestine: Its Historical Geography*, by Rev. Archibald Henderson, D.D., published by T. and T. Clark, Edinburgh. Geikie's *New Testament Hours* is a late publication, and describes in the author's fascinating style many of the present customs of the country. Whitney's *Handbook of Bible Geography* is a cheap and valuable work; as is also Hurlbut's *Manual of Biblical Geography*. Of lives of Christ, the very best for those who want facts rather than rhetoric is Andrews's *Life of Our Lord*. Other inexpensive works are Farrar's, Geikie's, and Stalker's. One should have a good Bible Dictionary, like Smith's. A book I would not be without is Baedeker's *Palestine and Syria*. It is the best guide book of the country, and is the inspiration, if not the foundation, for most of the books of travel on Palestine. The only objection to it is its high price. All these books can be secured through Eaton & Mains, New York, Boston, Pittsburg, Detroit, and San Francisco; or Curts & Jennings, Cincinnati, Chicago, and St. Louis. Even though one cannot provide himself with any or all of these helps, enough, it is hoped, is given in these pages to make the trip interesting and profitable.

It may be proper to say a word regarding the procuring and mounting of pictures for use in the class. Whatever you do, *do not show pictures from a book*. Curiosity will be too great to resist the temptation of examining other pages than the one shown, and thus the effect will be spoiled. The best pictures of Palestine are those in *The Land of Christ* and *The Earthly Footsteps of the Man of Galilee*. Some good views are to be found in the Stoddard series, *Glimpses of the World*. Old books, magazines, time-tables, etc., will furnish many valuable views. The large pictures in *The Land of Christ* are about eight by ten inches in size. These should be carefully trimmed and mounted on cardboard of sufficient thickness to prevent warping. The regular size of cardboard is twenty-two by twenty-eight inches. Have the printer cut each

Preface.

sheet in four parts, which will give the proper size for the eight by ten pictures.

A good paste, which is sufficiently adhesive and cheap, is a desideratum. I use a paste made of two tablespoonfuls of laundry starch, mixed with the white of one egg, and boiled for three or four minutes, stirring briskly to prevent lumps. This paste will not curl or warp the board. There are a great many brands of prepared paste. I have used successfully " Higgins's Photo-Mounter," a six-ounce bottle selling for twenty-five cents. Do not be discouraged if the first attempts at mounting are not successful. A little practice will enable one to mount as neatly and rapidly as the expert.

One word more : This little book would grow into volumes if all interesting points were discussed in full. *It is suggestive only.* The teacher must fill in the details, adapting all to the needs of the particular class of minds under direction. Maps should be drawn on the blackboard and places located as the itinerary progresses. The words and acts of Jesus should come in at their proper place in the narrative, with the background of earth and sky, of river, lake, wilderness, and mountain faithfully represented. Toward the close of the Lord's life the events themselves will become of surpassing interest, because every spot of ground on which he treads will be so familiar, and the peculiar customs and habits of the people so well known that everything will unite to make him the one object of vision and of thought.

WILLIAM E. McLENNAN.

Berwyn, Chicago, 1896.

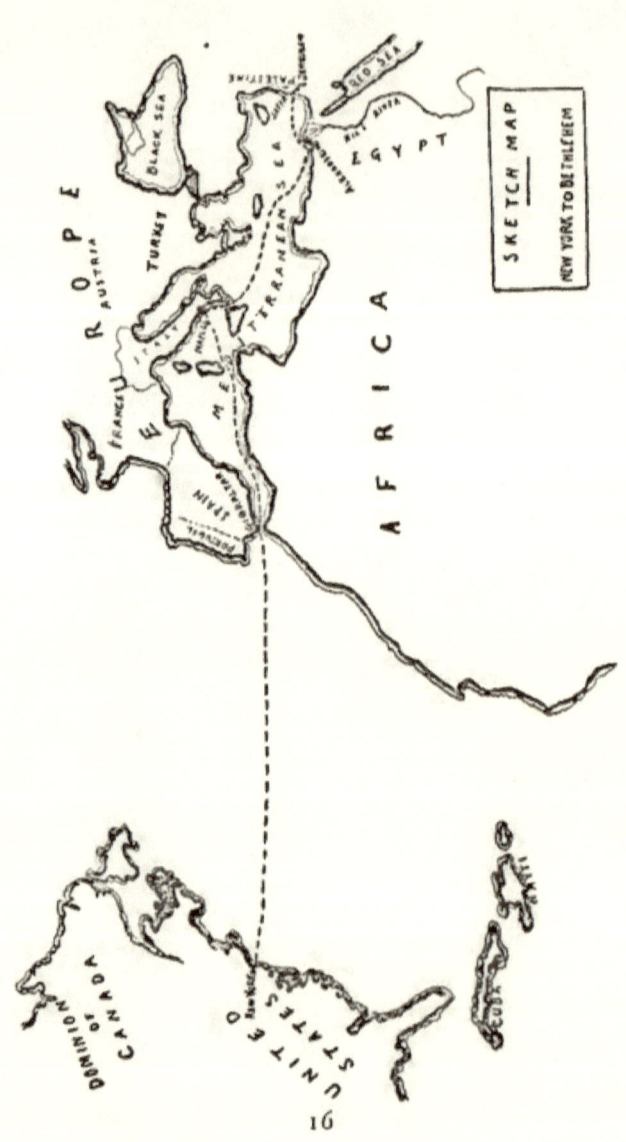

IN HIS FOOTSTEPS.

CHAPTER I.

Over Sea to Bethlehem.

ITINERARY AND MAP OF ROUTE FROM NEW YORK TO BETHLEHEM.—Leave New York by one of the steamers of the North German Lloyd Line—Gibraltar—Naples—Alexandria—Jaffa (Palestine)—Jerusalem—Bethlehem.

FROM NEW YORK TO GIBRALTAR.

HAVING arrived at New York we shall need to spend some time in selecting the special articles needed for our long journey. We have time enough and should not hurry. We should attend first to our outfit of clothing. Everything worn next the skin should be of wool and of the best material. Shoes should be broad-soled and not too thick or heavy. Ulsters and shawls of good quality and stout mackintoshes will be needed. Each person should have two suits of clothes, "one light in color for traveling, and a darker suit for visiting consuls, attending divine services, etc. The tailor should be instructed to make the sewing extra strong, for repairs are dear in the East, not to speak of the difficulty of finding the tailor just when he is wanted. Travelers will scarcely be inclined to adopt oriental costume; to do so without considerable familiarity with the language would only expose one to ridicule." For the head a pith helmet with a "puggery," or piece of muslin to protect from sunstroke, should be chosen. The complete change of climate experienced in passing from America to the far East will be apt to affect health unfavorably, hence a medicine case stocked with such remedies as quinine, made up into pills or capsules, cal-

In His Footsteps

omel, castor oil, opium in pills, an eye wash, ammonia, antiseptic wool, sublimate tablets, iodoform, collodion, etc., will be found of great service. There are a number of miscellaneous articles that should not be forgotten. The list should include a field-glass, a drinking-cup of leather or metal, notebooks, pocket compass, thermometer, and, if possible, a photographic outfit. Other materials we may safely leave until arrival in the East.

Before we embark we shall naturally wish to see something of New York itself, as it is not only the largest city in America, but is "next to London the most important commercial center in the world." It is almost entirely surrounded by water. On the west is the North or Hudson River; on the

S. S. LAHN, OF THE NORTH GERMAN LLOYD LINE.

east, East River; on its southern extremity, New York Upper Bay. Jersey City lies on the west, and Brooklyn on the east. Both the North and East Rivers are filled with vessels of all descriptions. The principal street is Broadway, which divides the city in the center. There are a multitude of interesting sights, too numerous even to mention; but, though we may not see them all, we shall take time to run through Central Park and to visit the station on Ellis Island, where immigrants from all portions of the world—from Palestine even—are landed almost daily. We shall locate some of the docks and observe where we may take our steamer for our long Atlantic trip.

At last the day has come to embark. Our state-rooms have been chosen and our baggage has been safely packed and

Over Sea to Bethlehem

stowed away. Our friends, if they have come to see us off, are on the pier waving us a last good-bye. We can hardly keep back the tears as we think of the dear land we are leaving, and of those who shall think of us and pray for us every day until we return after our long tour. We have already passed out into "The Narrows." Brooklyn Bridge and the Battery, and the great statue of "Liberty Enlightening the World" on Bedloe's Island, are fading out of sight. We pass Sandy Hook, and are upon the bosom of the great Atlantic.

The trip across the ocean changes very little from day to day. Occasionally porpoises, sharks, whales, and other sea monsters are seen. As we gradually move southward flying fish rise on both sides of our steamer, resembling flocks of snowbirds. The numerous vessels that hover in sight from day to day, laden with the commerce of many nations, suggest a fraternity of the sea which is one of the evidences that Christ has lived and that his Gospel is at work leavening the nations. After we are out a couple of days and get our "sea legs," as the sailors say, we will be deeply interested in examining our floating home. We shall make visits to the engine rooms, the steerage, the servants' quarters, etc. On fine days we shall find the ship's officers ready to give us any reasonable information about ships in general and our own ship in particular. As we must meet strange peoples in the Far East it will be interesting and profitable to study human nature about us. In traveling we find people at their worst and best. A good storm will try us all sufficiently, so that we may know just how earnest we are to go on with our expedition.

With favorable winds we sight the first dim outline of coast in about ten days. Not long afterward Gibraltar, the guardian of the Mediterranean, appears, resembling, at first, a great cloud that has settled upon the horizon. We watch it eagerly as our vessel draws nearer and nearer its rugged sides. Gibraltar is both a fortress and a town. It is the most southern extremity of Spain and belongs to Great Britain. It controls the entrance to the Mediterranean, and no ship may therefore pass it without permission of the English garrison. The so-called Rock of Gibraltar is about two and a half miles long and from one fourth to three quarters of a mile wide. The eastern side is too precipitous to be scaled, while all other points are protected with forts and batteries.

Gibraltar was known to the Greeks and Romans as the limit

In His Footsteps

of the world on the west. In the eighth century the Moors chose it as a fortress. It passed from one party to another until, in the sixteenth century, Spain so strengthened it that it was not taken until the war of the Spanish Succession, when Sir George Rooke hoisted the English flag in 1704. Seventy-five years later the combined fleets of France and Spain besieged Gibraltar, investing it for four years. The English garrison held out, and from that time no one has disputed England's control.[1]

FROM GIBRALTAR TO NAPLES.

We pass through the Straits of Gibraltar—some forty miles long—and are on the blue waters of the Mediterranean, or "Great Sea." No body of water in the world has so great his-

GIBRALTAR.

torical interest as this. The ships of Phœnicians, Egyptians, Greeks, Romans, and Carthaginians, of almost every nation of antiquity, have plowed its waters. Though our Lord doubtless saw it from afar, it is not probable that he ever sailed upon it.

---

[1] See a delightful description of Gibraltar by Dr. Buckley in *Travels in Three Continents*, pp. 103-116.

Over Sea to Bethlehem

We might have chosen the route by way of Malta and Port Said, the latter situated at the entrance of the Suez Canal. This would make our trip somewhat shorter; but, on the whole, the opportunity of visiting Naples, one of the most charming cities of Italy, and the historic Alexandria will more than compensate for the added time and distance.

We shall not see in our entire trip, nor should we see, if we traveled around the globe, a finer view than Naples, with its volcano and its far-famed bay, presents. A well-known proverb describes the feelings of the most enthusiastic visitors: "Vedi Napoli e poi mori" ("See Naples and die"). But we shall not despair, for we are not in search of beauty, which is often associated with the most disgusting vices, a fact illustrated in Naples itself, but we follow the footsteps of One who, while he loved beauty, spoke only of truth and righteousness.

FROM NAPLES TO ALEXANDRIA.

We get several views of Italy and of many well-known islands, while our ship heads for the African coast. We shall read much about what we see and ask many questions. This, together with a proper interest in our strange fellow-passengers, will occupy most of our spare time. Before reaching Alexandria we shall find that we have sailed on the Mediterranean alone something over two thousand miles, occupying the better part of two weeks.

Egypt! What visions crowd upon us of pyramids, sphinxes, mummies, of ruined temples and tombs! But we cannot think of such things now. We are in New Egypt. Alexandria was founded in 332 B. C. by Alexander the Great, and for a considerable time rivaled in magnificence Antioch and Rome. At the beginning of the present century it had almost fallen into decay. To-day we find a practically new city of about two hundred thousand inhabitants, one fourth of whom are Europeans. A half day's carriage ride will show us the most important sights, such as Pompey's Pillar, the Palace of the Khedive, etc.

FROM ALEXANDRIA TO JAFFA.

We may have our choice of three lines of steamers from Alexandria to Jaffa, those of the Messageries Maritimes, Austro-Hungarian Lloyd, the latter sailing every alternate Friday, or an Egyptian line. The first two touch at Port Said.

In His Footsteps

Unless we are particularly anxious to spend a few days at Port Said, on the Suez Canal, it will be best for us to take the Egyptian line direct for Jaffa.

We are now in sight of the land made sacred by patriarchs and prophets, especially by Him who was both Son of man and Son of God, our Saviour, Jesus Christ. Our long journey to the land of Christ is about ended. In a few hours we shall stand on the sacred soil of Palestine. Above us lies Jaffa, or Yafa, as it is called by its own citizens, a city of about twenty-five thousand inhabitants. We cannot land as in the splendid harbors of our own country, but must come to anchor, and then reach the town by means of small boats. "The debarkation at Jaffa, as

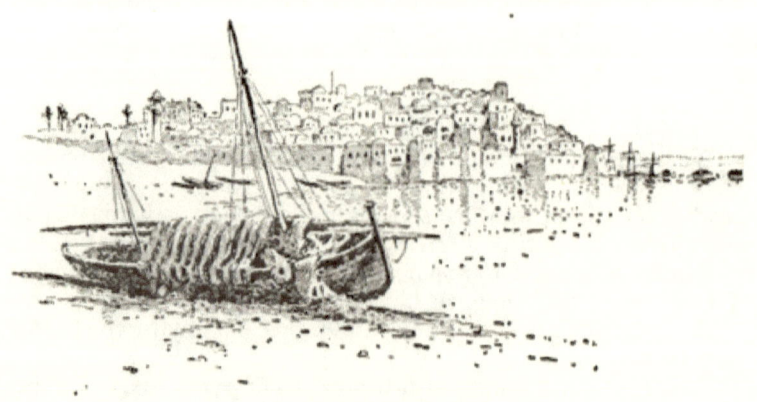

JAFFA FROM THE NORTH.

everywhere in the East, is invariably conducted with the least possible order and the greatest possible noise." Boatmen with strange gestures and a stranger speech importune us for patronage. To those who are particularly noisy we may say a few words like "*Iskut*" ("Be quiet"), "*Imshi*" ("Begone"), which, with certain significant gestures, will clear a way for us from our steamer to the small boat we have engaged to transfer us to the shore. On our way we are reminded that this is the site of the ancient Joppa, "to which Hiram, King of Tyre, undertook to send to Solomon wood from Lebanon 'in flotes' for the building of the temple." From this very spot the prophet Jonah took ship for Tarshish when disobedient to the command of God. Here, on a housetop, Peter saw that vision

Over Sea to Bethlehem

(Acts ix, 36-43; x, 9) which helped him to overcome his prejudices against the Gentiles.

Our boat has touched the shore, and we are, at last, upon the sacred soil of Palestine. We pass the custom house, and on up through the crooked streets of the town to the Jerusalem Hotel, whose proprietor bears the suggestive name of Hardegg. It is regarded as a good stopping place. We are all ready for a good rest, after which we shall see something of the town and complete arrangements for our journey through the country.

Though Jaffa is not a large city, and differs in some respects from other towns of Palestine, it is sufficiently characteristic to serve as a type of the rest. The streets, we find, are narrow, "often so much so that the roughly projecting upper story, or stories, seen here and there, are close together, shutting out both light and heat. The narrowness is, indeed, designed to secure this, for the sun smites sorely in these warm lands, and shade is a necessity as well as a delight in the heat of the day. But the want of 'made' roads leaves everything very wretched under foot. In the hot weather the dust is inches deep, and, for this, in the rainy season, the equally deep mud is a poor exchange. Shops are mere recesses, with no glass or front of any kind, the goods being displayed in what answers to the window space, a large part of which, however, is often taken up by the shopkeeper himself, squatted with his feet under him among his wares." As we proceed we must gradually get accustomed to the obnoxious stenches, for sanitation is something unknown in Eastern towns. The habit of doing nearly everything out of doors almost entirely does away with privacy. "In Eastern towns all trades are carried on largely in the open air, from shaving to hammering out copper trays or bowls, and we may be sure it was the same in Palestine in the days of our Lord. Even the dentist performed, more or less, in the open street, and, just as one has to do to-day, our Lord would have to tread his way through a crowd of people on foot, mechanics busy at their callings, or riders on asses, and not seldom would have to get out of the way of a huge camel, stalking slowly through the confusion. For it is to be remembered that there are few pavements [sidewalks] for those walking; everyone goes where he sees a possibility of progress, whether he be riding a donkey or leading a gigantic camel, *and the East never changes.*"[1]

[1] Geikie, *New Testament Hours.*

In His Footsteps

At Jaffa we shall be obliged to complete our arrangements for the tour through the country; hence it will be necessary not only to select our mode of traveling, but to learn something of the people, so that we may not needlessly intrude upon them, nor carelessly violate any of their cherished opinions. Too often the traveler imagines that he may act just as he does in his own country, without any regard to the views of the people with whom he mingles. Three things every traveler should cultivate, especially in the East—thoughtfulness, courtesy, firmness.

There is but one completed railroad in Palestine—that which runs from Jaffa to Jerusalem. Very soon a road will be finished from Haifa farther up the coast, eastward to Damascus, skirting the southeastern shore of the Sea of Galilee. Our trip will be so extended that we shall choose to make arrangements for transportation other than by rail. As roads are so few in Palestine, carriages are out of the question. We are left, therefore, to the choice of horses or camels or to going on foot. The latter we would hardly undertake. Some would select camels without hesitation for the novelty of riding on such an animal. But while "he commands our respect, and even our admiration, he rarely gains our affection;" and respect and admiration are apt to grow less and less every day he is used as a means of locomotion. Horses are very much to be preferred to camels. "Oriental horses are generally very docile, and may therefore be safely mounted by the most inexperienced rider." "Travelers who are unacquainted with the language and customs of the country will find a dragoman (or manager) indispensable." Having selected our dragoman, we can make arrangements with him for providing us with all necessary equipment, such as tents, etc. He will also act as interpreter and general manager of the expedition. We shall take a tent, though in the larger towns we shall find hotels, and in almost all places *hospices* in charge of monks, representing the various Christian Churches. There are no restaurants in Palestine, but cafés, where coffee and other light refreshments are served, abound.

The present population of Palestine, which is not above two millions, consists of *Franks*, or Europeans; *Jews*, the most of whom are recent settlers from Europe; *Syrians*, "descendants of all those peoples who spoke Aramaic at the beginning of our era, with the exception of the Jews;" *Arabs*, consisting

Over Sea to Bethlehem

of settled and nomadic or wandering tribes; *Turks*, whose numbers are not large, but on account of their relation to the government have certain privileges not granted to others.

The inhabitants are divided according to religious belief into Mohammedans, who make up four fifths of the whole population; Christians, made up of Greek and Roman Catholics and Protestants; and Jews. The Mohammedan belief is that "There is no God but God, and Mohammed is the prophet of God." Mohammedanism is the prevailing religion in Palestine. Mohammedans "generally wear white turbans with a gold thread woven in the material. The Christians are also distinguishable by their costume. In the towns they generally wear the simple red fez, which is occasionally enveloped in a dark turban. The Jews are generally tall and slender in stature, wear their peculiar sidelocks of hair and broad-brimmed felt hats or turbans of dark cloth."

A JERUSALEM JEW.

In all intercourse with the natives of the country we should be careful to observe what they regard as proper form. "Orientals accuse Europeans of doing everything the wrong way, such as writing from left to right, while they do the reverse, and uncovering the head on entering a room, while they remove their shoes, but keep their heads covered. The traveler should endeavor to habituate himself to the custom of taking off the shoes on entering a house, as it is considered a grave breach of politeness to tread upon the carpets with

In His Footsteps

them." We must, while in the East, become accustomed to great delays. Time means nothing with these people. They are very ceremonious in their reception, entertainment, and dismissal of guests, and so patience is very much needed. Still, as we proceed, we shall become accustomed to their ceremony and rather enjoy it. One thing we cannot fail to mark, that "the degraded ruffianism so common in the most civilized countries is quite unknown here. The people of the country, even of the poorest and entirely uneducated class, often possess a native dignity, self-respect, and gracefulness of manner, of which the traveler will grieve to admit his own countrymen, of a far higher status in society, are for the most part utterly destitute."

AN ARAB.

We may as well, right in the beginning, make up our minds not to rely altogether on the English language. We shall need to learn something of the Arabic, which is universally spoken. One word will meet us everywhere, and ring in our ears as we depart—the word "*Backsheesh.*" It means "a gift," and as everything is to be had for gifts the word has many applications. "Thus with backsheesh the tardy operations of the custom-house officer are accelerated, backsheesh supplies the place of a passport, backsheesh is the alms bestowed on a beggar, backsheesh means blackmail, and, lastly, a large proportion of the officials of the country are said to live almost exclusively on backsheesh." The natives regard every traveler as a Crœsus. "In every village the traveler is assailed with crowds of ragged, half-naked children shouting, '*Backsheesh, backsheesh, ya khowaja!*' The best reply is to complete the rhyme with '*Ma fish, ma fish*' ("There is nothing"), which will generally have the effect of dispersing them."

Over Sea to Bethlehem

FROM JAFFA TO JERUSALEM.

Everything having been arranged with our dragoman, we set off in good season for that city whose name and history will live longest with the race—Jerusalem, the type and symbol of our heavenly home. It is but forty-one miles from Jaffa. We pass through the Jerusalem Gate and turn toward the southeast, passing high cactus hedges with orchards behind them. We pass the house of Tabitha (Acts ix, 36), the plain of Sharon, Lydda a little to our left, Ramleh, founded about 700 B. C., and Ajalon, where Joshua commanded the sun to "stand still upon Gibeon," and the moon "in the valley of Ajalon." There are numerous other places identified with towns and villages of Scripture, but we cannot pause to examine them. From Kuloniyeh, four and one half miles from Jersusalem, which some identify with Emmaus, we begin to ascend, finding our road gradually becoming more and more stony and dreary. At last the glittering dome of the Mosque of Omar, which has taken the place of the temple, bursts upon our view, and "behind it the tower of the Mount of Olives," on the opposite side of the city. Dome after dome of the churches and mosques appear, and, finally, the city's walls. In a few minutes we have passed the Jaffa Gate and are within the city.

HIGHWAY WITH CACTUS HEDGE.

What is now called Jerusalem, we soon learn, is not the

In His Footsteps

city over which Christ wept. That has long since passed away. It lies buried under the dust of centuries. The present city is inclosed by a wall some forty feet in height, surmounted by thirty-four towers. The walls are pierced by eight gates, one of which is closed, the principal one being the Jaffa Gate through which we have just entered. Jerusalem is not a pleasant city, though not unhealthful. Lawns, yards, and parks are a rarity. The most of the streets are not ten feet in width, and are irregularly paved. Everything is covered with oriental dirt. The population is not much above forty thousand. More than half are Jews. The remainder are about equally divided among Mohammedans and Christians. Of the latter four thousand are orthodox Greeks, two thousand are Latins, less than five hundred are Protestants. There is much to see in Jerusalem, but we shall reserve the chief objects of interest until subsequent visits, as we follow our Lord's footsteps during his early life and later ministry.

AN ORIENTAL STREET.

Over Sea to Bethlehem

FROM JERUSALEM TO BETHLEHEM.

We pass out of Jerusalem at the same gate by which we entered and turn southward on one of the best roads in Palestine. It is but six miles to Bethlehem. Passing through the upper part of the Valley of Hinnom we cross a plain, probably the Valley of Rephaim, where David met and defeated the Philistines (2 Sam. v, 18). A little farther along is a cistern known as the "Well of the Magi," where it is said the wise men saw the star after their departure from the presence of Herod (Matt. ii, 9). One of the most interesting sights on the road between Jerusalem and Bethlehem is the so-called "Tomb of Rachel," which is supposed to mark the scene of Rachel's death (Gen. xxxv, 19). The spot is equally sacred to Mohammedan, Christian, and Jew. Here we turn to the left from the main road, and in less than a quarter of an hour are in the outskirts of Bethlehem.

BETHLEHEM—FROM THE VALLEY OF THE SHEPHERDS.

We have, at last, like those ancient worshipers from the East —the Magi—found the place where the young child was born. From this point our real pilgrimage begins, for we are to walk the same ground, so far as we can, which he passed over from his birth to his ascension.

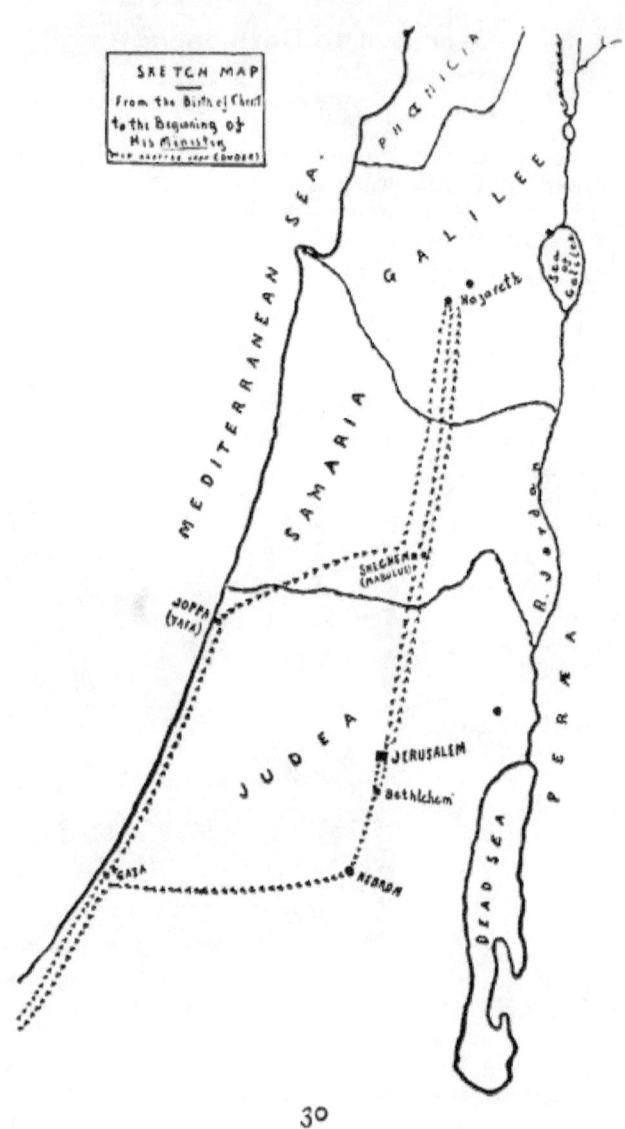

From Birth of Christ to Beginning of Ministry

CHAPTER II.

From Birth of Christ to the Beginning of His Ministry, B. C. 5–A. D. 27.

ITINERARY AND MAP.—Birth of Christ at Bethlehem—Jerusalem —Egypt, through Bethlehem—Hebron, Gaza—Jerusalem— Nazareth.

IN BETHLEHEM.

Birth of Christ, December, B. C. 5,	Luke ii, 6, 7.
Adoration of the shepherds, . .	Luke ii, 8–20.
Circumcision, ...	Luke ii, 21.

BETHLEHEM is a very old town. It is here where Naomi and Ruth lived. It was the home of the family of David, and within it David was crowned King of Israel. The prophet Micah declared that the Messiah should be born here (Micah v, 2). The town lies on "the eastern brow of a ridge that runs from east to west, a mile in length, and is surrounded by hills." It is two thousand five hundred and fifty feet higher than the level of the Mediterranean. The present population is about eight thousand, of whom two hundred and sixty are Mohammedans and but fifty are Protestants. "A walk down the main street of Bethlehem must bring before us as close a reproduction of an old Hebrew village of Christ's days as we can hope to see, though perhaps it is less sordid, from the influence of Western ideas. There is no thought of sanitation, in the Western sense. Rivulets and puddles of abomination abound, and the long-nosed, yellow, masterless dogs cannot eat all the garbage. The workshops are only arches with no window—the busy workers sitting crosslegged on the floor, carving rosaries, perhaps from the stones of the dôm palm, or of the date or olivewood; or crosses of various materials; or ornaments of bitumen from the Dead Sea; or cutting Scripture scenes on oyster shells from the Red Sea. Nothing could be ruder than the place in which they work, for it is often a rough cave, with a layer of reed stalks overhead to keep out the damp; the natural limestone left uncarved as a floor, and the doorway an illustration of carpentry primitive enough for the prehistoric period. Shops there may be said to be none, but men sit on the ground along the sides of the streets with piles of vegetables for sale; or dusty groceries spread out on a few boxes or rough shelves; or a small stock of raisins, oranges, or figs; or cakes and thin sticks of bread; or a tempting assortment of mouse-traps, and other equally important attractions. It was much the same, no doubt, when Joseph and Mary came to Bethlehem, nineteen hundred years ago, finding shelter, one may fancy, where the Church of the Nativity now stands, with its bare open space in front, and

BETHLEHEM—"THE CHURCH OF THE NATIVITY" IS SURMOUNTED BY A CROSS.

children play and old men rest on fallen ancient pillars that lie here and there. The line of the two or three streets, the character of the houses, and the names of the people are still, no doubt, virtually the same as when Christ lay a babe in the Bethlehem manger."[1]

The object of all interest in Bethlehem is, of course, the great "Church of St. Mary," or, as it is generally known, the "Church of the Nativity." There is a tradition as far back as the second century that Christ was born in a cavern.

[1] Geikie, *New Testament Hours.*

From Birth of Christ to Beginning of Ministry

There is nothing in the record against such a belief. Caves were used for many purposes. "Perhaps the fact may be that the cave, in its original shape, was connected with a house,

THE CHAPEL OF THE NATIVITY.

forming its rear apartment and used as a stable. To this house went Joseph and Mary, when they could find no room

In His Footsteps

at the inn, and when the child was born it was laid in the manger as the most convenient place."[1] Over this cavern, which has been believed all these centuries to be the birthplace of Christ, the Emperor Constantine built a church in the year 330. It is believed that the present edifice is the original structure. At any rate, it is the oldest church in the world. But it is not the magnificent church as much as the " Chapel of the Nativity " that interests us. This chapel is the Cave of the Nativity, and is about forty feet long, twelve feet wide, and ten feet high. The pavement and linings of the walls are of marble. Under the altar is a recess around which burn fifteen lamps. In the center of the recess is a silver star with the inscription: *"Hic de Virgine Maria Jesus Christus natus est"* (" Here Jesus Christ was born of the Virgin Mary"). Three steps below is the " Chapel of the Manger," where it is said the original wooden manger was discovered by the Empress Helena. There are many other objects of interest pointed out, but it might as well be said that the majority are manufactured, not having even the uncertain basis of tradition.[2]

We can imagine the shepherds hurrying in from the plain within a few minutes' walk of Bethlehem to look upon the face of the newborn Child. These were not ignorant men like those we generally meet to-day among the peasantry, but probably guardians of the flocks for the use of the temple.

Regarding the rite of circumcision, it is an open question whether it was performed in Bethlehem or Jerusalem. Geikie thinks the Child was taken to the temple as it was so near, but there is nothing in proof of such a statement. "Custom would allow of its being done in the local synagogue, or in the humble house of prayer, in Bethlehem itself, or even in the house in which Joseph and Mary lodged."

FROM BETHLEHEM TO JERUSALEM.

Presentation in the temple, ... Luke ii, 22-33.

From Bethlehem Jesus is carried up to Jerusalem to be presented to the Lord in the temple. On our way we may glance at the peculiar characters we meet, the various styles

---

[1] Andrews, *Life of Our Lord.*
[2] Photographs of paintings by the old masters may easily be secured for illustration of Christ's birth.

From Birth of Christ to Beginning of Ministry

of garments, and the types of beasts of burden. Just such a scene must have met the eyes of Joseph and Mary as they went up to the temple according to the custom of their nation. As they approached the city the first object to attract them would be the temple itself. They would pick their way through the crowded streets, narrow and dirty, as now, into the sacred inclosure, where they would dedicate their firstborn to the service of God. What lessons of consecration do we learn as we follow them into the city! But what a change has taken place! There on Mount Moriah the original temple was built by Solomon, rebuilt by the command of Cyrus, 516 B. C. The temple in which our Lord was pre-

JERUSALEM—THE MOSQUE OF OMAR.

sented was begun by Herod, B. C. 20, and destroyed by the Romans, A. D. 70. On the site of that temple there now stands a Mohammedan mosque—the Mosque of Omar. It is thus described by Rev. J. M. Buckley: "The Mosque of Omar, built over the rock, and often spoken of as the Dome of the Rock, is a splendid building, octagonal in shape, each side being sixty-six feet long, having gates facing each of the points of the compass. On entering I gazed about me with awe. The light came dimly through thirty-six stained glass windows, when suddenly the sun, emerging from a cloud, lighted up the dreadful gloom, which oppressed the mind and pained the

In His Footsteps

eye, and the long cloisters appeared. We stood upon a pavement of elegant marble mosaic, and above us rose a dome to the height of ninety feet, having a diameter of sixty-six feet. The walls are covered with tiles of every hue, of priceless value, and the frieze consists of tiles which bear inscriptions from the Koran."

FROM JERUSALEM TO EGYPT BY WAY OF BETHLEHEM, HEBRON, AND GAZA, B. C. 4.

Visit of the Magi,	Matt. ii, 1-12.
The Flight,	Matt. ii, 13-15.

There is much difference of opinion as to the order of events. Some think the visit of the Magi, or wise men, came before the presentation in the temple; others believe that, after the visit at Jerusalem, the family went to Nazareth, where the wise men sought them. There is no evidence on which a positive opinion can be based. The weight of opinion favors the order here indicated.

Again we are on the road from Jerusalem to Bethlehem, passing southward. Somewhere on the road—tradition says at the "Well of the Magi"—the wise men saw the star, after their departure from Herod. They followed the star, and according to the traditional belief, which seems reasonable, they found him in Bethlehem and presented him with their gifts—gold, frankincense, and myrrh.

On account of the determination of Herod that no one shall rise to dispute his authority as "King of the Jews;" Joseph and Mary are warned to depart into Egypt. The traditional route of the family to Egypt was from Bethlehem south to Hebron, thence west to Gaza, and southwest through the desert to the village of Matariyeh, near Cairo. There are many interesting sights on the way, and the opportunity of looking upon the childhood home of our Lord will be well worth the time and effort necessary to make the trip. From Bethlehem it will take about one and a quarter hours to reach the Pools of Solomon, directly south. These pools are immense tanks made of large hewn stones coated with cement. It is believed that they were built in Solomon's time to furnish water for the temple. Hebron is about as far from Solomon's Pools as the Pools are from Jerusalem. It is a very ancient town, rivaling Damascus in this respect.

¹ *Travels in Three Continents.*

From Birth of Christ to Beginning of Ministry

There is a tradition that here Adam was created. Sarah, the wife of Abraham, died at Hebron. It was destroyed by Joshua (Josh. x, 27), and was an important center during David's life. The present town has about five thousand inhabitants, nearly all Mohammedans, and very fanatical, as we discover when the children follow us shouting Arabic curses. From Hebron we turn southwest to Gaza, which has

IN THE LAND OF EGYPT—RAISING WATER FROM THE NILE FOR IRRIGATION.

many Egyptian characteristics. Gaza is an important trading center between Egypt and Palestine. Near the town we visit the spot that is pointed out as the place from which Samson carried off the gates of the Philistines.

The journey of Joseph, Mary, and the Babe to Egypt occupied, according to tradition, two weeks. We shall hardly make the trip in less time now. Arriving at Matariyeh we shall find many evidences of what tradition has marked as memorials of the holy family's visit. The Nile, with its peculiar boats, the Pyramids, Sphinx, etc., are very much what they were when Christ was in Egypt, though there is nothing to show that either he or his parents looked upon either the river or these ancient monuments.[1]

FROM EGYPT TO NAZARETH.

Leaving Egypt, ...	Matt. ii, 16-23.
Boyhood in Nazareth, ...	Luke ii, 40.

It is impossible to say how long the family remained in Egypt. Authorities vary from a few months to eight years. They were there until the message came, "They are dead that sought the young child's life." In all probability they expected to return to Nazareth by way of Jerusalem, but when Joseph heard that "Archelaus was reigning over Judea in the room of his father Herod, he was afraid to go thither [to Jerusalem], and being warned of God in a dream he withdrew into the parts of Galilee." They may have reached Nazareth following the coast northward as far as Jaffa, thence northeast to Shechem, or what is now Nabulus, thence directly north, on the Nazareth and Jerusalem road, to their home. Without positive knowledge of the route, we can only choose that which seems the most reasonable.

TENT LIFE IN PALESTINE.

Second only in interest to the place of the Lord's birth is Nazareth, where he spent his boyhood, that period which usually determines what the rest of life shall be. How eagerly we scan those streets which so closely resemble the very ones in which Jesus played and over which he often walked on some errand for his parents! But we cannot examine them now. Our horses need food, and particularly rest after their long journey from the south. The best camping ground is among

---

[1] Dr. Buckley's *Travels in Three Continents* gives an interesting account of Egyptian antiquities. They are well illustrated in *The Earthly Footsteps of the Man of Galilee*.

From Birth of Christ to Beginning of Ministry

those orchards on the north of the town. We shall put up our tent and prepare for quite a long visit. Had we arrived in the spring we would have found its white walls "embosomed in a green framework of cactus hedges, fig and olive trees."

Nazareth, whose present name is En Nasira, is not mentioned in the Old Testament. The question that was often asked, "Can any good thing come out of Nazareth?" is a hint that its reputation was not very good. However, there is no place so bad but that, if it is God's will we should be there, we may, as did Christ in Nazareth, live a holy life. The present population is seven thousand five hundred, made

NAZARETH.

up principally of Orthodox Greeks, Latins, and Mohammedans. There are about two hundred Protestants. Every one visiting Nazareth seeks some memorial of Christ. We turn our steps to the great Latin monastery on the east of the town. Inside its high walls is the "Church of the Annunciation." Two columns in the chapel of this church mark where the angel Gabriel and Mary are supposed to have stood when it was announced that she was to be the mother of Christ. On the rock, which is overlaid with marble, it is said the "House of the Virgin" stood. There is a story told that on May 10, 1291, this sacred dwelling, that it might not be desecrated by impious hands, was carried by angels into Dalmatia, and thence to Italy. A little north of the monastery we come to the so-called house and workshop of Joseph. Ascending the hill on the northwest we get a fine view of the town and

In His Footsteps

surrounding country. On the east is Mount Tabor and Little Hermon, southwest is Mount Carmel and the Mediterranean, directly south the famous plain of Esdraelon. We need not doubt that from this very point the boy Jesus saw just what we see to-day. On the east as we descend is a spring called St. Mary's Well. The pilgrims of the Greek Church bathe their eyes and head in this water, believing it to be sacred. There is no other spring in Nazareth. Standing there we see at evening crowds gather with pitchers to draw water, and can almost believe ourselves looking upon a scene such as Jesus saw many a time in this his own town.

Besides these memorials of Christ, tradition has given us many stories of his boyhood. It is told of him that he carried water in his robe; pulled a short board to the required length; molded sparrows out of clay which flew when he clapped his hands; turned his playmates into kids; struck dead the boys who ran against him in play. Of course, all such stories are vulgar inventions. Nobody who possesses common sense believes them. From all we read in the gospels we have no reason to believe that Jesus was different from the majority of boys except in his perfect obedience to his parents, his kindness to his playmates, his lack of all rudeness to the aged or others, and his love of service. He was a *perfect boy*, loving and beloved, just such a character as any boy may resemble if he will. He played as well as worked, and his laugh was probably as loud as that of any boy in Nazareth; but we may be sure he never laughed at sorrow or pain or old age, nor listened to anything that was coarse or vulgar.

FROM NAZARETH TO JERUSALEM, A. D. 8.

On the road, ... Luke ii, 41, 42.
In the temple, ... Luke ii, 43-50.

When Jesus was twelve years of age his parents decided to take him with them to Jerusalem to attend the annual passover or festival. How anxiously he must have looked forward to such a journey! All boys like to visit a large city, and are always interested in the sights on the way. "His presence at the passover, at the age of twelve, was in accordance with Jewish custom. At that age the Jewish boys began to be instructed in the law, to be subject to the fasts, and to attend regularly the feasts, and were called the Sons of the Law."[1]

---

[1] Andrews, *Life of Our Lord;* also Meyer and others.

From Birth of Christ to Beginning of Ministry

Jerusalem is about eighty miles from Nazareth, and the journey takes about three days of easy travel. Joseph, Mary, and Jesus, together with their neighbors, must have taken the road, or rather path (as roads according to our Western ideas are unknown in Palestine), through Samaria, notwithstanding the bitterness between Samaritans and Jews. Crossing the plain of Esdraelon on the south we get a fine view of Mount Tabor to the northeast, pass Jezreel, now called Zerim, where Saul lost his life fighting his great battle against the Philistines (1 Sam. xxix, 1 ; 2 Sam. i, 21). "Jezreel was afterward the residence of King Ahab and of Jezebel. On the vine-clad hills lay the vineyard of Naboth, where Joram, Ahab's

GALILEAN CARAVAN APPROACHING JERUSALEM.

second son, was slain by Jehu." The attention of the boy Jesus was, doubtless, called to these interesting events in the history of the chosen people. Our next important town, following the steps of the family on to Jerusalem, is Jenin. This was unknown in Christ's time, unless it answered to the ancient Engennim (Josh. xix, 21). Past Jenin the road skirts Samaria, now known as Sebastiyeh, once the capital of the kingdom of Israel. Here John the Baptist, according to tradition, was buried, and Philip preached the Gospel. The next important town on our route—indeed, one of the most important towns in Palestine—is Nabulus (Nablus or Nablous). It is on the site of ancient Shechem. On one side

In His Footsteps

of the town is Mount Gerizim, and on the other is Mount Ebal, famous in Old Testament history for their relation to the giving of the law. Then, as now, Mount Gerizim was the holy mountain of the Samaritans. Climbing the mountain we discover a little basin near the summit where the Samaritans pitch their tents during the celebration of the feast of the passover. Just out of Nabulus we pass Joseph's tomb and then Jacob's well, where, a few years later, Jesus speaks of the water of life to the "woman of Samaria." The only other places worthy of attention before reaching Jeru-

JESUS AND THE DOCTORS.
(From the painting by Holman Hunt.)

salem is Seilun, the ancient Shiloh—the home of Eli and Samuel (1 Sam. iii and iv)—and Betin or Bethel. The history of all these places must have been referred to as the family passed on to the capital. Nearing the city they would see vast crowds, greater by many thousands than ever attended the Columbian Exposition at Chicago, covering all those hills. Josephus reckoned the number attending a single passover at more than two and a half millions. "Every house in the narrow limits of Jerusalem was crowded with pilgrims, and the whole landscape round covered with tents

From Birth of Christ to Beginning of Ministry

or booths of mat and wickerwork and interwoven leaves. As Joseph and Mary with her son came in sight of the city from the north they would be on ground as high as Mount Zion," which lay in front of them a little to their right, overtopping the other hills on which the city is built. On its summit they would see Herod's palace. With what eagerness would the boy's eyes be turned to the left, where, on Mount Moriah, stood the temple, with the fortress of Antonia near it! Below him, to the south, was the lower city. All around Jerusalem are valleys which, with the neighboring hills, are practically unchanged since the eyes of Jesus first rested upon them. On the west and south are the valleys of Gihon and Hinnom, north and east the valley of Jehoshaphat and the bed of the brook Kedron. On the east is the Mount of Olives, with the garden of Gethsemane on its western slope. To-day we see Mount Zion given over to the Armenians, and Mount Moriah, which now bears the name of Haram esh Sherif, is crowned by the Mohammedan Mosque of Omar. Sad as these changes seem, we can, if we try, imagine ourselves in the Jerusalem of the days of Jesus. On that holy mount of Moriah he entered his Father's house for the first time since he was brought there as a babe to be dedicated to God. Now he was a "Son of the Law," and might perform all religious duties. "The tephillin, or phylacteries, had doubtless, as was usual, been put on him publicly in the synagogue of Nazareth, to mark the transition from boyhood, to remind him that he was henceforth to wear them, to keep the feasts, to follow the law of the rabbis, and to think seriously of his future calling in life. He would be freer, therefore, to go where he liked, without supervision, than a boy of the same age with us, and hence all Jerusalem, with its thousand wonders, lay before him to study as he chose."[1]

FROM JERUSALEM TO NAZARETH.

Return, ... Luke ii, 51a.
Stay in Nazareth until beginning of public ministry, . . Luke ii, 51b, 52.

We retrace our steps northward over the same route which brought us to Jerusalem. Many objects of interest not before observed will meet us on the way. How often Jesus

---
[1] Geikie, *Life of Christ*.

In His Footsteps

walked this road previous to his entrance upon his ministry we do not know, but it was doubtless very familiar to him.

From his return after his boyhood visit to Jerusalem his youth, as his boyhood, was spent in the quiet home at Nazareth. These must have been years full of blessing. Here he prepared himself in body, mind, and heart for his ministry. "The white, flat-roofed houses of to-day are, doubtless, much the same as those amidst which he played as a child and lived as a man; vines shading the walls; doves sunning

INTERIOR OF A PEASANT'S HOUSE.

themselves on the flat roofs; the arrangements within as simple as they are unpretentious without. A few mats on the floor; a built seat running along the wall spread with some modest cushions and the bright quilts on which the inmates sleep at night, and serving by day as shelf for the few dishes in common use; a painted chest in the corner; some large clay water jars, their mouths filled, perhaps, with some sweet herbs to keep the contents cool and fresh; the only light that entered, by the open door; a low, round, painted wooden stool, brought at meals into the middle of the room to hold the tray and dish, round which the household sat, with crossed knees, on mats, supply the picture of

From Birth of Christ to Beginning of Ministry

a house at Nazareth of the humbler type."[1] He must have read the Old Testament again and again, until its great truths became a part of his deepest life. And then he was often, we may believe, upon those hills about Nazareth, looking into the peaceful valleys and toward those glorious mountain peaks which seemed to tell him so much of God.[2] But he was no day dreamer, no idler. He worked faithfully in Joseph's shop, learning the most valuable lessons while mending a neighbor's plow or helping to build a village house. From such a life, with its leisure and its toil, with its simplicity and its sublimity, he goes out to preach to all who will hear him the Gospel of the kingdom.

[1] Geikie, *Life of Christ*.

[2] "Across Esdraelon, opposite to Nazareth, there emerged from the Samaritan hills the road from Jerusalem, thronged annually with pilgrims, and the road from Egypt, with its merchants going up and down. The Midianite caravans could be watched for miles coming up from the fords of Jordan; and the caravans from Damascus wound round the foot of the hill on which Nazareth stands. Or, if the village boys climbed the northern edge of their hollow home, there was another road within sight, where the companies were still more brilliant—the highway between Acre and Damascus, along which legions marched and princes swept with their retinues and all sorts of travelers from all countries went to and fro."—George Adam Smith, *The Historical Geography of the Holy Land.*

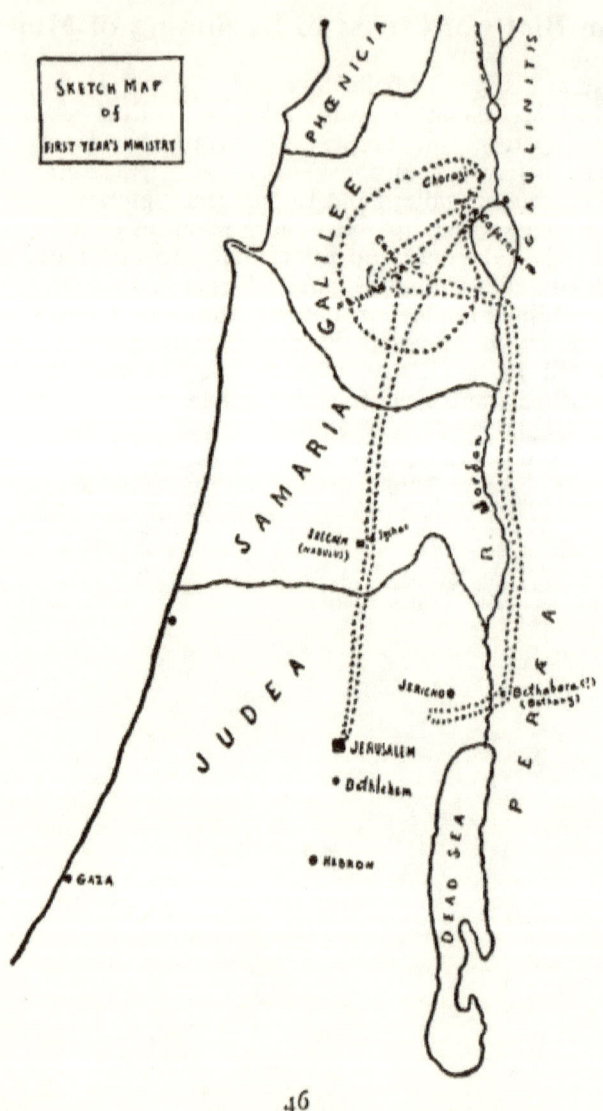

First Year's Ministry

CHAPTER III.

First Year's Ministry, January to December, A. D. 27.

ITINERARY ON MAP.—Nazareth to Jordan—Wilderness—Cana—Capernaum—Jerusalem—Cana through Judea and Galilee—Nazareth—Capernaum—Circuit through Galilee—Capernaum.

FROM NAZARETH TO THE JORDAN.

Baptism of Jesus,[1].   Matt. iii, 13-17; Mark i, 9-11; Luke iii, 21, 22.

THE route which Jesus chose to the Jordan is not known, though it is not unlikely that he crossed to the east side of the river, just south of the Sea of Galilee, and followed it down to the place where John was baptizing. According to the gospel of John (i, 28) the scene of the baptism was Bethabara, or Bethany (not the Bethany east of Jerusalem), but there is no means of knowing its exact location. Almost every conceivable opinion is held by one or more scholars. The majority place it just north of the Dead Sea, almost directly east of Jericho. "The place (five miles northeast of Jericho) was known as Bethabara (Bethany), 'the house of the ford.' Fords do not change in a river like the Jordan; roads are never altered in the East; and this must always have been, as it is now, the place of passage from Jericho to Gilead.

"This was the ordinary place of passage for those who traveled from Galilee to Jerusalem by the Jordan route. Here our Lord often crossed with his disciples when he

---

[1] The passover which our Lord attended this year (A. D. 27) fell on April 9. It would seem, therefore, that his baptism could not have been much earlier than January. The point, however, is scarcely worthy of discussion, particularly as no one has scarcely anything more than conjecture on which to base an opinion regarding the chronology of our Lord's life. The writer has no desire to discuss, even if he were qualified for such a task, the respective merits of the "tripaschal" and "quatripaschal" theories. Personally he accepts the scheme which makes the ministry of Christ between three and four years in length. For the order of events, especially the opening ministry, Stevens's and Burton's *Analytical Outline*, as representing the views of the majority of biblical writers and scholars, is closely followed. As to dates, Andrews is believed to represent as reliable a classification as any, though he is not regarded as by any means infallible.

In His Footsteps

would avoid passing through Samaria on his way to the temple festivals at Jerusalem."[1] The route from Nazareth following the Jordan is not unpleasant. The valley of the Jordan, from the Sea of Galilee to the Dead Sea, is from six hundred and fifty to thirteen hundred feet below the level of the Mediterranean. "It is filled up to a certain level with alluvial deposit, forming what is often called the 'upper plain' of the Jordan valley; and in this the river has hollowed out for itself during the course of long ages a 'lower plain,' varying in width from a quarter of a mile to a mile, and from

THE JORDAN—WHERE JOHN BAPTIZED.

fifty to one hundred feet below the general level of the valley."[2] In Christ's time this eastern side of the Jordan had a much larger population than now. Christ was going down to meet John, by whom he would be baptized. "On baptism, in itself, he put no mysterious sacramental value. It was only water, a mere emblem of the purification required in the heart and life, and needed an after baptism of the Holy Spirit. No one could receive it until he had proved his sincerity by an humble confession of his sins. Baptism then be-

[1] Tristram.   [2] Wilson.

First Year's Ministry

came a moral vow, to show, by a better life, that the change of heart was genuine."[1]

FROM THE JORDAN TO THE WILDERNESS.

Temptation of Jesus, ... Matt. iv, 1-11; Mark i, 12, 13; Luke iv, 1-13.

The scene of the Lord's temptation was in the wilderness of Judea. Some, with Stanley, believe the "wilderness" referred to was on the eastern side of the Jordan; others hold, with Pressensé, that it was on the western shore of the Dead Sea. "Those denuded rocks, that reddened soil scorched by a burning sun, that sulphurous sea stretching like a shroud

THE WILDERNESS OF JUDEA.

over the accursed cities, all this land of death, mute and motionless as the grave, formed a fitting scene for the decisive conflict of the Man of Sorrows." Still others will agree with Porter, that the temptation took place just west of Jericho. "No man who stands on the banks of the Jordan at Jericho

[1] Geikie, *Life of Christ*.

In His Footsteps

could doubt for a moment where that wilderness is. He has only to lift up his eyes and look westward, and it is before him. . . . The wilderness of Judea, including the whole of that wild region lying between Jericho and Jerusalem, was unquestionably the scene of the temptation." This is in accordance with the traditional belief, and may be accepted until there is more evidence than mere opinion to disprove it. "A bare, white plain, with two or three narrow strips of verdure, extends about six miles from the west bank of the river. On its farther side rises up a ridge of white limestone cliffs, extending north and south as far as the eye can see, and supporting a chain of jagged, rocky hills behind, equally white and bare. A more dreary, desolate, and forbidding landscape the world could not furnish." Surrounded thus, does it not seem that our Lord was most severely tried? To us everything would have seemed as though we had been abandoned of God.

FROM THE WILDERNESS TO CANA, BY WAY OF THE JORDAN.

Testimony of John the Baptist, ... John i. 20-36.
Choice of five disciples, ... John i. 37-51.
The marriage feast at Cana, ... John ii. 1-11.

After his temptation the Lord returned from the wilderness to the Jordan, probably at the same place where he had been baptized. We therefore retrace our steps, crossing to the east side of the river, and imagine as we come up on the other side hearing the voice of the great prophet as he says of Jesus, "Behold the Lamb of God that taketh away the sin of the world." Two of the Baptist's disciples, Andrew and probably John, the author of one of the gospels, hearing these words, follow Jesus. The next day Simon Peter becomes a disciple, and the day following Philip, a townsman of Andrew and Peter, is brought to Christ. Philip finds Nathanael, a resident of Cana in Galilee, and says to him, "We have found him, of whom Moses in the law and the prophets did write." The Lord is on his way north to Cana. His probable route was the road east of the Jordan, by which we came south following him to his baptism.

There are now two Canas in Galilee, Kanet (or Kana) el Jelil, situated about twelve miles north of Nazareth, and Kefr Kenna, four miles northeast. Most authorities agree that Kefr Kenna is on the site of the ancient Cana, and there we shall

First Year's Ministry

go. It lies in a small valley on the edge of a plain. "At the entrance of the village is a fountain made out of an ancient sarcophagus, which the inhabitants show as the fountain from which the waterpots were filled."[1]

Our stay in the country will have, to some extent, prepared us to understand the nature of that marriage feast at Cana. To-day, among the Mohammedans, after the marriage contract is arranged, and "before the wedding, the bride is conducted in gala attire and with great ceremony to the bath. This procession is called 'zeffet el-hammam.' It is headed by several musicians with hautbois and drums of various kinds; these are followed by several married friends and relatives of the bride in pairs, and after these come a number of young girls. The bride is entirely concealed by the clothing she wears, being usually enveloped from head to foot in a cashmere shawl, and wearing on her head a small cap or crown of pasteboard. The procession moves very slowly, and another body of musicians bring up the rear."[2] It is very suggestive of the spirit with which our Lord began his work that his first recorded miracle is at a wedding, thus indorsing marriage and justifying the innocent joy that accompanied it.

FROM CANA TO CAPERNAUM.
John ii, 12.

Why Jesus went to Capernaum at this time we do not know. Some think that his family had removed there from Nazareth. Possibly he visited it on the invitation of Peter and Andrew, "who seem now to have resided there." Of one motive that led him to make the trip we need have no doubt. Coming to save sinners he would naturally go where men and women were congregated in large cities. Capernaum was not far from Cana, seventeen miles in a straight line, or about twenty by the usual road. As we see it now it is a vast ruin, but in the Lord's day it was a stirring town "of fisher people, grain and fruit agents, local tradesmen, and the many classes and occupations of a thriving station on a great line of caravan traffic. The daily business of Capernaum itself supplied many of the illustrations so frequently introduced into the discourses of Jesus. He might see in the bazaar of the town, or on the street, the rich traveling merchant, who exchanged a heavy load of

---
[1] Andrews, *Life of Our Lord.*   [2] Baedeker, *Palestine and Syria.*

In His Footsteps

Babylonian carpets for the one lustrous pearl that had, perhaps, found its way to the lake (the Sea of Galilee) from distant Ceylon. Fishermen and publicans and dressers of vineyards passed and repassed each moment. It was this town, on the border between the districts of Philip and Antipas, by the shore of the lake, in the midst of thickly sown towns and villages, that Jesus selected as his future home."[1] Much

RUINS OF CAPERNAUM.

of that life is suggested by what we see to-day on and around the Sea of Galilee: "The casting of nets; the abundant supply of fish; the scattered flocks; the sheep which follow the good shepherd; the lilies of the field in abundance; the sea, often tempestuous, and all the old-time natural surroundings."[2] But the glory of those early days has all departed. The fields are not tilled, the thriving towns and cities have degenerated into squalid villages, the inhabitants seem to have no ambition for anything except a bare existence. The only attraction is the memories of Jesus.

[1] Geikie, *Life of Christ*.
[2] Edward L. Wilson, *The Sea of Galilee*. Century Magazine for December, 1887.

First Year's Ministry

FROM CAPERNAUM TO JERUSALEM, APRIL, A. D. 27.

First cleansing of the temple,	John ii, 14-22.
Performs many miracles,	John ii, 23-25.
Visited by Nicodemus,	John iii, 1-21.

The time for the annual passover is at hand, and Jesus, with his disciples, goes up to Jerusalem. We assume that he took the same road on which it is believed he walked as a boy of twelve. It is again the month of April, the most charming season of all the year in Palestine. Should we be so fortunate as to follow our Lord's footsteps southward in that month we should see, as Jesus did, "the plains covered with rich

HEROD'S TEMPLE.

green, and the gray hills lit up with red anemones, rock roses, red and yellow, the convolvulus, marigold, wild geranium, red tulip, and a hundred other glories." As Jesus approached Jerusalem he would see the hills covered with the multitudes pressing their way toward the city. He himself crowded his way with his Galilean friends toward the temple. His visit there as a boy of twelve would be fresh in his mind. Now he is a man almost thirty, with more than a man's work to do. What does he find in the temple, which nearly eighteen years before he had referred to as his "father's house?" "There, in the actual court of the Gentiles, were penned whole flocks of sheep and oxen, while the drovers and pilgrims stood bar-

In His Footsteps

tering and bargaining around them. There were the men with the great wicker cages filled with doves, and under the shadow of the arcades, formed by quadruple rows of Corinthian columns, sat the money changers, with their tables covered with piles of various small coins. And this was the entrance court to the temple of the Most High! The court which was a witness that that house should be a house of prayer of all nations had been degraded into a place which, for foulness, was more like shambles, and for bustling commerce more like a busy crowded bazaar; while the lowing of oxen, the bleating of sheep, the babel of many languages, the huckstering and wrangling, and the clinking of money and of balances (perhaps not always just) might be heard in the adjoining court, disturbing the chant of the Levites and the prayer of priests."[1] "Entering the polluted temple space, and gazing round on the tumult and manifold defilements, he could not remain impassive. Hastily tying together some small cords, and advancing to the sellers of sheep and oxen, he commanded them to leave the temple, with their property, at once, and drove them and their beasts out of the gates. The sellers of doves were allowed to take their cages away, but they, too, had to leave. The money changers fared worse, as they deserved. Their tables were overturned, and they themselves expelled."[2,3] After long years the temple was once more sacred to God."

On these streets the Lord performed his many miracles. In some quiet corner Nicodemus had his interview with Jesus, and learned what were the necessary conditions for gaining entrance into the kingdom of God.

FROM JERUSALEM JESUS DEPARTS INTO JUDEA, AND THENCE TO GALILEE THROUGH SAMARIA.

Baptizes in Judea (through his disciples),	John iii, 22.
Leaves Judea,	John iv, 1-4.
At Jacob's well,	John iv, 5 26.
In Sychar,	John iv, 27-42.
Arrival in Galilee,	Luke iv, 14.

How long Jesus was in Judea at this particular time, and what points he visited, we have no means of knowing. Some

---

[1] Farrar, *Life of Jesus Christ*.   [2] Geikie, *Life of Christ*.
[3] The expulsion of the money changers cannot but be deeply interesting to young people, and may be used as an opportunity for imparting many valuable lessons. Questions

First Year's Ministry

think that he went to the Jordan; others believe that "he went from place to place baptizing wherever he found water, and that he visited in southern Judea, Hebron, and the chief cities, going as far south as Beer-sheba." Still others hold to the opinion that his work was in the northern part of Judea. He may have been at Wady Farah, some six miles northeast of Jerusalem, where is abundant water. In the

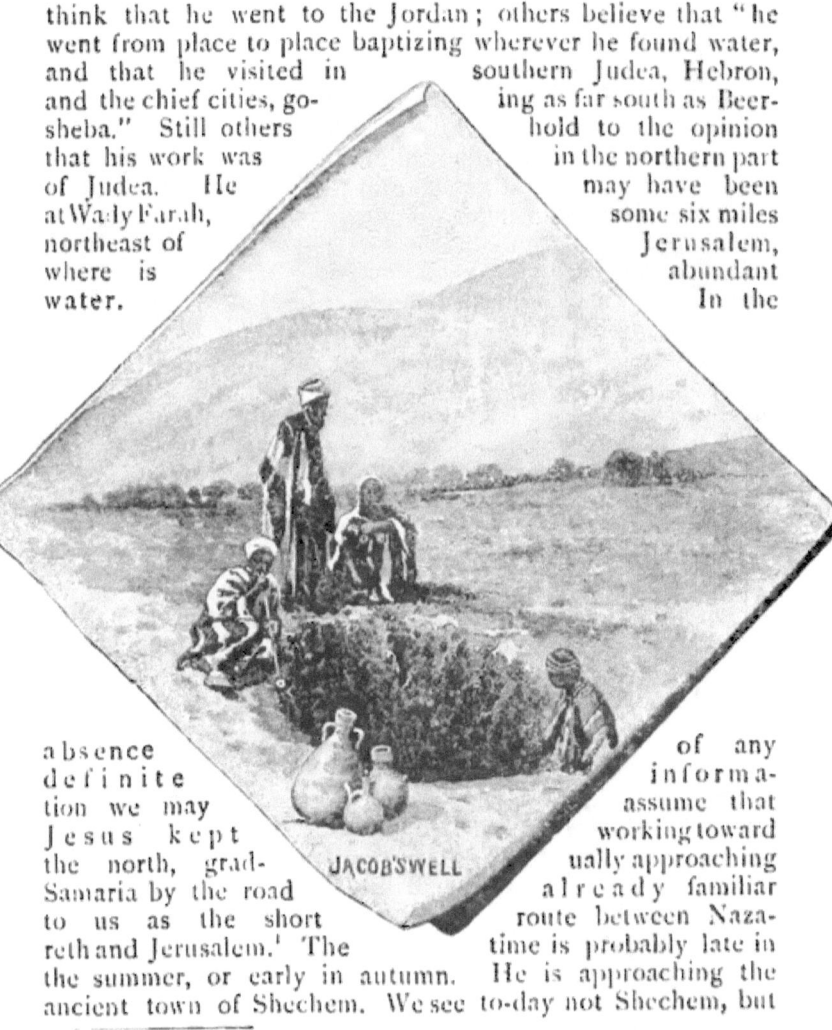

JACOB'S WELL

absence of any definite information we may assume that Jesus kept working toward the north, gradually approaching Samaria by the road already familiar to us as the short route between Nazareth and Jerusalem.[1] The time is probably late in the summer, or early in autumn. He is approaching the ancient town of Shechem. We see to-day not Shechem, but

---

like the following will bring out the most essential truths: Is it wrong to collect money in the Lord's house for any purpose? What kind of people were engaged in this huckstering? For whose advantage were they so engaged? Is it ever right to buy and sell merely for *private* gain? What does Christ's act in cleansing the temple reveal of his physical strength? of his spiritual zeal? Who are the strongest, the physically or the morally strong?

[1] It has already been noted that the Jews usually preferred the roundabout way on the east of the Jordan so as to avoid the hated Samaritans.

In His Footsteps

Nabulus. "Luxuriant gardens, richly watered, girdle it round outside its old dilapidated walls, whose gates, hanging off their hinges, are an emblem of all things else in this day in Palestine." ... "But before Jesus came to the town he halted for a time to rest. Close under the eastern foot of Mount Gerizim, at the opening of the side valley from the wide plain, on a slight knoll, a mile and a half from the town, surrounded now by stones and broken pillars, is Jacob's well."[1] All agree that this is the identical well on whose edge the Lord sat while he talked to the "woman of Samaria" of the water of life. The woman came not from Shechem (Nabulus), but Sychar, "which is probably identical with the modern Asker." The woman came about the noon hour with a water jar upon her head, and "a long cord in her hand with which to let the jar down the well." This well must have been noted for its good water in Christ's day, for it was then very deep. Even to-day it is seventy-five feet in depth. "To get at the mouth of the well one must be let down into the vault that has been built over it."

There is not much left of Asker, the ancient Sychar, where the woman lived. There are some rock tombs and a spring. When Christ visited the town it was evidently a thriving village.

On his arrival in Galilee Jesus is cordially received by the people on account of his labors in Judea.

THROUGH GALILEE TO CANA.

Heals the nobleman's son, ... Luke iv. 46-54.

The Lord may have hastily passed through Nazareth on his way north, though it is not probable. The report of his coming to Cana has preceded him, and finally reaches the ear of a nobleman in Capernaum—perhaps Herod's steward, Chuza—whose son is lying at the point of death. Palace walls cannot keep out God's messengers of warning, neither can they prevent Christ's blessed influences reaching the remotest corner.

FROM CANA TO NAZARETH, A. D. 28.

Rejected, ... Luke iv, 16-30.

It is believed by some, whose ability and scholarship are unquestioned, that Jesus, after living a short time in retire-

[1] Geikie, *Life of Christ*.

First Year's Ministry

ment, went up to Jerusalem, and afterward returned to Nazareth. The majority of writers, however, agree that he went to Nazareth immediately after healing the son of the nobleman at Capernaum.

The road from Cana to Nazareth is very familiar to us now, as it evidently was to Jesus. He wanted his neighbors to receive him as the Messiah, but they would not admit his claims. To them he was only the son of the carpenter. On a certain Sabbath he went into a synagogue, " as his custom was." Jesus never neglected the house of worship.'

In our wanderings about Nazareth we shall see the " Mount of Precipitation," from which it is popularly believed the inhabitants of Nazareth tried to cast our Lord.

FROM NAZARETH TO CAPERNAUM.

The journey,	Matt. iv, 13-16; Luke iv, 31.
Selects four apostles,	Matt. iv, 18-22; Mark i, 16-20; Luke v, 1-11.
A day of miracles,	Matt. viii, 14-17; Mark i, 21-34; Luke iv, 31-41.

From Nazareth the Lord, rejected by those of "his own city," goes down to Capernaum, passing Cana on the way. From this time on, for a considerable period, Capernaum becomes his headquarters. The present village of Tell Hum and its surroundings are all that mark the Capernaum of our Lord. " The place consists of a dozen miserable huts. There are a number of black ruins in the center " of which we can trace the remains of a beautiful ancient building resembling marble. Some think these are the ruins of the synagogue standing in Christ's day.

The call to " Follow me," given to Andrew and Peter, James and John, at the Jordan was the call to discipleship. That is now followed by the summons to become the foundation stones of " the kingdom." These men were fishers. Boats, nets, the lake had been familiar to them from childhood.

How blessed a Sabbath to the large number who were healed in Capernaum! Christ's Sabbath day activity shames our indolence! The one day in the week best adapted for reaching the souls of men the average Christian almost wholly wastes, imagining that if he does no positive harm he is keeping the Sabbath day holy.

---
[1] Visit a synagogue the next time you are in a city and persuade some intelligent Jew to explain the differences between Jewish customs now and in early days.

In His Footsteps

Peter had a house in Capernaum, and it was a favorite resort of Jesus and his immediate followers. It probably resembled many of the houses we now see in our travels in Palestine—bare walls, earthen floor, no windows, fireplaces and chimneys unknown, as "the floor serves for chairs and table, and a mat on it for a bed. The flat roofs, reached by a coarsely made stair at the side, have their clay dovecotes, and serve at some seasons as cool sleeping places, shelters of boughs being set up to keep off the night winds and the moonshine.

FROM CAPERNAUM JESUS MAKES A CIRCUIT TO THE "NEXT TOWNS," RETURNING TO CAPERNAUM.

Matt. viii, 2-4. Mark i, 35-45. Luke iv, 42-44; v, 12-16.

Among the towns which the Lord visited were doubtless those nearest Capernaum—Chorazin and Bethsaida—though he probably passed through many others. On this journey he performed many miracles, but the only one recorded is the healing of a leper. His name was now in everyone's mouth, great crowds following him from place to place. On our trip through Galilee to-day we see scarcely anything to remind us of the times of Christ except the earth and sky. Going north from Capernaum we pass over a succession of ruins, volcanic rocks and lava, which many think mark the sites of the ancient cities of Chorazin and Bethsaida. It is anything but easy this journey through Galilee, but it was no less difficult for Jesus. He could restore a wrecked manhood in the person of the leper seeking his help,[1] but who will restore these ruined cities? Only a people touched with the spirit of Christianity—the spirit of hope and energy and determination.

AT CAPERNAUM, FOLLOWING CIRCUIT THROUGH GALILEE.

Heals the paralytic, . . . Matt. ix, 2-8; Mark ii, 1-12; Luke v, 17-26.
Calls Levi (Matthew), ... Mark ii, 13-17; Luke v, 27-32.

Back again in Capernaum with its ruins! What seems to us in America a very hard, almost an impossible, thing appears very easy in Palestine, namely, the uncovering of a roof. It is "only a few feet high, and by stooping down and holding the corners of the couch—merely a thickly-padded quilt, as at present in this region—they could let down the sick man

[1] See any Bible Dictionary for a description of leprosy.

First Year's Ministry

without any apparatus of ropes or cords to assist them. And thus, I suppose, they did. The whole affair was the extemporaneous device of plain peasants, accustomed to open their

EASTERN HOUSE—SHOWING FLAT ROOF AND COURT-YARD.

roofs and let down grain, straw, and other articles, as they still do in this country."[1]

Just outside the city there was, in the Lord's time, a "receipt of customs," where a representative of the Roman government received taxes. The Jews were very bitter against Rome, and especially hated the tax. He who collected this "custom" was called a publican, and if he chanced to be a Jew he was more despised by his countrymen than if he were a citizen of Rome. Such a man was Levi (or Matthew), yet the Lord called him to be his follower; for Jesus does not regard our outward appearance or our employment, but only our hearts.

---
[1] W. M. Thomson, *The Land and the Book.*

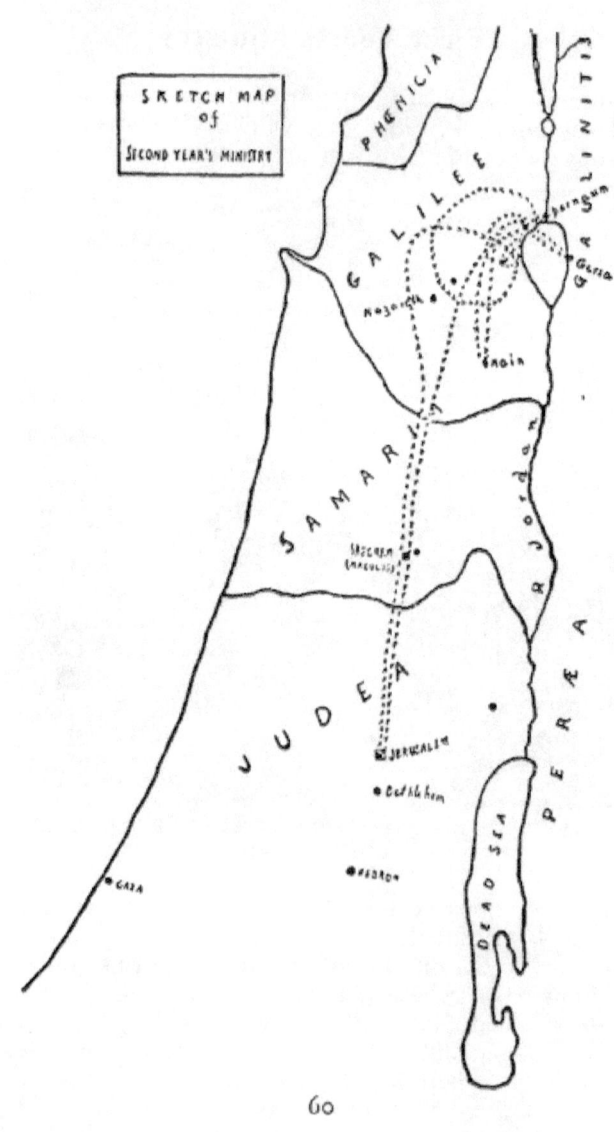

Second Year's Ministry

CHAPTER IV.

Second Year's Ministry, January to December, A. D. 28.

ITINERARY ON MAP.—Capernaum—Jerusalem—Return to Galilee and the Sea—Mount of Beatitudes—Capernaum—Nain—Capernaum—Circuit of Galilee, returning to Capernaum—Across the Lake to Gersa—Return to Capernaum.

FROM CAPERNAUM TO JERUSALEM.[1]

Heals an infirm man at Pool of Bethesda, ... John v, 1-16.
Replies to the Jews, ... John v, 17-47.

ANOTHER journey southward through a country very familiar to us now. There is much doubt where the "Pool of Bethesda" was located, though modern excavations seem to place it "a little northwest of the Church of St. Anne, and not far from the present St. Stephen's Gate." This gate is on the eastern side of the city opening to the *Via Dolorosa*, or street of pain, "the route by which Christ is said to have borne his cross to Golgotha." On the right, as we enter, right by the gate, is St. Anne's Church. The ground on which this church stands was presented to Napoleon III by the Sultan Abdul Mejid at the close of the Crimean war. The reservoir or pool, formerly known as the Pool of Bethesda, whose waters were thought to heal diseases, is cut thirty feet into the solid rock. "There were twenty-four steps originally cut in the rock, and thus it would be very difficult to get down to the water."

FROM JERUSALEM TO GALILEE.

The disciples pluck grain, arousing the hostility of the Pharisees, . Matt. xii, 1-8; Mark ii, 23-28; Luke vi, 1-5.
Jesus cures the man with the withered hand, . . . Matt. ii, 9-14; Mark iii, 1-6; Luke vi, 6-11.

The Lord was so much opposed in Jerusalem that he concluded to return to Galilee. Doubtless he took the familiar

---

[1] As before stated, there is no unanimity among scholars as to the time when Jesus made this journey to Jerusalem. If we knew what feast this was which Jesus attended—Purim, Pentecost, Passover, Tabernacles, Day of Atonement, Trumpets, or Woodgather-

In His Footsteps

road to the north. On a certain Sabbath—at what place in Galilee we do not know—as they were walking along, fields on both sides of them and no fences, the disciples, being hungry, began to pluck a few heads of wheat which they rubbed in their hands to separate the kernels from the chaff. We might do the very same thing to-day, and nothing would be thought of it. The Pharisees did not object to the disciples taking the wheat, for that was allowable, but to the rubbing of the heads. To do that was equal to threshing, so the Pharisees believed or pretended to believe. Jesus showed them their great mistake. It was not wrong to take and prepare food on the Sabbath. Besides, he was Lord of the Sabbath day. How earnestly he must have studied the Scriptures to speak so clearly of David and of the temple and its service!

The higher lesson of the Sabbath Christ teaches in the healing of the man with the withered hand. What is the Sabbath for? It is a day of rest; but it is also a day of opportunity for doing the greatest good, not for quibbling over technicalities. The Pharisees were always thinking about what they could not do. Christ came to show us how much we can do if we have his spirit. The healing is done in the synagogue, the house dedicated to the worship of God. Our frequent visits to the temple and synagogue, following our Lord's footsteps, ought to impress us deeply with the Saviour's regard for the house of prayer.

CROSSING THROUGH GALILEE JESUS GOES TO THE SEA— GREAT MULTITUDES FOLLOWING HIM.

Matt. iv, 23-25; xii, 15-21; Mark iii, 7-12.

As we pass through Galilee we are struck with the great changes which have taken place in the character and number of the population since the day when the multitudes from all the towns and provinces surrounding the Sea of Galilee eagerly sought after Jesus to hear him and see his mighty works. Then there were numerous towns in Galilee, the smallest, according to Josephus, numbering not less than fifteen thousand people. The Lake of Galilee was covered

---

ing—we should not find much trouble in settling the other questions involved. But the gospels do not say which of the numerous feasts it was. Most recent writers believe it was the passover, and so make the Lord's ministry nearer four than two years. Andrews, though believing this feast was the passover, puts the rejection at Nazareth after the Lord's return from this visit to Jerusalem.

Second Year's Ministry

with ships engaged in fishing and traffic, and its shores were dotted with cities and villages. To-day, as we wander along those shores, we find only ruins and desolation.

FROM THE SEA OF GALILEE TO THE MOUNT OF BEATITUDES.

Spends the night in prayer, ... Luke vi, 12.
Chooses the twelve, ... Mark iii, 13 to; Luke vi, 13-19.
"Sermon on the Mount," . . . Matt. v, vi, vii; Luke vi, 20-49.

There is much difference of opinion over the location of the mount where Jesus prayed all night, and from which he afterward delivered the so-called Sermon on the Mount. Some think that all that can be legitimately drawn from the

THE HORNS OF HATTIN—PROBABLE SCENE OF "THE SERMON ON THE MOUNT."

narrative is that our Lord went upon any one of the mountain ridges surrounding the Sea of Galilee; but there are others, with more show of proof, who hold that it was a particular mount, and there is none which seems so likely to be *the mount* as what is known as *Kurn Hattin*, or "Horns of Hattin." "It is a hill with a summit which closely resembles an oriental saddle with its two peaks." This hill lies on the road between the cities of Tiberias and Nazareth. From the thirteenth century it has been known as the "Mount of Beatitudes." From this eminence we see, looking toward Nazareth, a broad and undulating plain; on the east are numerous cliffs, and right below us lies the village of Hattin. Beyond the village we look upon a "wild and tropical gorge,"

In His Footsteps

and farther away the shining waters of the Sea of Galilee. It was, in all probability, on one of these "horns" of the mount that Jesus prayed all night, and to this place he called the twelve, "that they should be with him." By this final choice of the apostles the kingdom was established. From this spot Jesus descended to the plain where the multitude had gathered, healed a number of the sick, and reascending gave the sermon, the twelve being about him and the people just below him.

FROM THE MOUNT OF BEATITUDES TO CAPERNAUM.

Crowds following,	Matt. viii, 5–13.
Heals the centurion's servant,	Luke vii, 1–10.
His condition alarms his friends,	Mark iii, 20, 21.

The distance from Hattin to Capernaum is not over seven or eight miles. On his arrival at Capernaum he is met by an embassy from a Roman centurion, sent to request him to come and heal the centurion's sick servant. Among the things named in the soldier's favor was his liberality in building a synagogue in the town. It is possible that the ruins of a synagogue which we now see in Tell Hum (Capernaum) are the remains of the identical building erected by the good centurion.[1]

So earnest, so intense is the Lord in his work, that his friends try to restrain him. They speak as though he were beside himself. Those whose souls are not on fire will always think the deeply earnest are mad.

FROM CAPERNAUM TO NAIN.

Restores to life a widow's son,	Luke vii, 11–17.
Receives a message from John the Baptist,	Matt. xi, 2, 3; Luke vii, 18–20.
Replies to John,	Matt. xi, 4–6; Luke vii, 21–23.
Addresses the multitude,	Matt. xi, 7–19; Luke vii, 24–35.

Nain is about twenty-five miles from Capernaum, southeast of Nazareth, and just off the Nazareth and Jerusalem road, at the foot of a mountain known as Little Hermon. The place now consists of wretched clay huts with rock tombs near. "Nain must have been a city; the ruined heaps and traces of walls prove that it was of considerable extent, and a walled town, and therefore with gates, according to the gospel narrative."[2] If Jesus left Capernaum early in the morning he would reach Nain early in the afternoon of the same day.

---

[1] See Andrews, Tristram, Edersheim, Colonel Wilson, and others. [2] Tristram.

Second Year's Ministry

To-day we see in our journeys through Palestine scenes similar to that in Nain when Jesus visited it. As soon as there is a death the body is immediately washed and within a few hours buried, provided the interment can be made before sunset. The procession to the grave is always accompanied with loud wailings. The bier on which the body of the young man was carried was doubtless "a mere open frame like that still used for such purposes in Palestine."

FUNERAL SCENE IN PALESTINE.

While at this little town of Nain, and after the restoration to life of this son, Jesus received John the Baptist's sad message asking if he was indeed the Christ. Could John have followed Jesus with the twelve, or have known what we now know, he would not have asked that question.

FROM NAIN TO CAPERNAUM.

Dines at the house of Simon the Pharisee, . . . Luke vii, 36-50.
Parable of the two debtors, ... Luke viii, 1-3.

It is in doubt whether the words recorded by Matthew (xi, 20-30) were spoken at Nain or later, and whether Jesus

In His Footsteps

returned directly from Nain to Capernaum or spent some time on the way teaching in the various towns in the neighborhood.

As soon as Jesus returned to Capernaum he was invited to the home of a Pharisee named Simon. As the Lord could not be anything else but courteous he did not refuse the invitation, though he well knew that the Pharisee was more eager to see him than to love him.

We can easily imagine the kind of a house to which Jesus was invited. "Raised divans or table couches, provided with cushions and arranged on three sides of a square, supplied a rest for guests, and on these they lay on their left arm with

TOMBS ON THE ROAD TO NAIN.

their feet at ease behind them, outside. A kiss on the cheek from the master of the house, with the invocation, 'The Lord be with you!' conveyed a formal welcome, and was followed, on the guest taking his place on the couch, by a servant bringing water and washing the feet, to cool and refresh them, as well as to remove the dust of the road and give ceremonial cleanness. The host himself, or one of his servants, next anointed the head and beard of the guests with fragrant oil, attention to the hair being a great point with orientals."[1]

As the houses were so much more open than ours it was easy for anyone to approach without violating any law of privacy. Jesus never put himself where it would be difficult for one seeking help to find him.

---
[1] Geikie, *Life of Christ*.

Second Year's Ministry

FROM CAPERNAUM THE LORD, ACCOMPANIED BY THE TWELVE AND CERTAIN WOMEN, MAKES A CIRCUIT OF GALILEE.

Returning to Capernaum, ... Luke viii, 1-3.

On that journey we cannot go, as there is no word to show what points Jesus visited.

On returning to Capernaum :

Heals one possessed of a devil, ... Matt. xii, 22.
Controversy with the Jews, ... Matt. xii, 23-45; Mark iii, 22-30.
His mother and his brethren, Matt. xii, 46-50; Luke viii, 19-21; Mark iii, 31-35.
At the shore, ... Matt. xiii, 1.
Enters a boat and teaches, . Matt. xiii, 2-52; Mark iv, 1-34; Luke viii, 4-18.
Conversation with a scribe and a disciple, . Matt. viii, 19-27; Luke ix, 57-60.

Jesus went to the shore of the lake at Capernaum, we may believe, that there might be more room for the crowd that persistently surged about him; but even there he was so

THE SEA OF GALILEE.

pressed upon that he was obliged to get into one of the little fishing boats moored near the shore. There he could speak without interruption. What he said is of the greatest importance, and here we have only to lift our eyes and look about us for illustrations of his teaching. There are the fields and the sower, the "tree" grown from the smallest of seeds, the woman making bread, the field with its hid treasure, the fisherman and his net, etc. All these were very familiar to the people whom Jesus addressed. To those visiting these scenes to-day there seems to come the echo of the Lord's words, so persistent is custom in the Far East.

In His Footsteps

FROM CAPERNAUM ACROSS THE SEA OF GALILEE TO THE COUNTRY OF THE "GERGESENES."

On the sea, ... Matt. viii, 18; Mark iv, 35-41; Luke viii, 22-25.
Casts out demons, . . Matt. viii, 28-34; Mark v, 1-20; Luke viii, 26-39.

The Lord's motive in crossing the lake was doubtless to escape the crowd, which must have wearied him greatly. The trip may have taken place early in the evening, or, as many think, at night. Where the "country of the Gergesenes" was has caused much discussion. It is now generally agreed that it was on the east side of the Sea of Galilee, at a place now known as Kersa, Chersa, or Gersa, exactly six miles southeast of Capernaum.

"In Christ's day whole fleets of boats found occupation on the lake; coasters, ferryboats, and boats for fishing. Josephus, indeed, a generation later, collected at one time no fewer than two hundred and thirty. Now, however, there seems to be only the simple boat in which I was rowed along the lake. Sharp at both ends, perhaps like that of Peter or James and John, it was about six or eight tons burden, with a mast of twelve or thirteen feet, raking forward; a rope through a pulley near the top serving to hoist a huge sail, if needed. At the stern it was decked for about five feet, and on this 'upper seat' a mat was laid down for me. Was it here that Christ lay during the storm, or was he contented to sleep on the planks below? He must often have had the same glorious view as I then enjoyed. Hermon, flashing light from its unstained snows, rose high into the northern heavens; lesser mountains, gradually sinking into the modest hills along the shore, reaching like a long train of attendants from the steps of this dazzling throne."[1] A storm was not an uncommon thing on the Sea of Galilee. It is six hundred feet lower than the Mediterranean, and its heated air rising meets the cold winds from Mount Hermon, producing heavy squalls. "Small as the lake is, and placid in general as a molten mirror, I have repeatedly seen it quiver and leap and boil like a caldron, when driven by fierce winds from the eastern mountains, and the waves ran high—high enough to fill or 'cover' the ships, as Matthew has it."[2]

Arriving at the eastern shore Jesus finds fierce demoniacs coming out of the tombs. In that same locality may be seen

---
[1] Geikie, *New Testament Hours*.   [2] Thomson, *The Land and the Book*.

Second Year's Ministry

to-day just such burial places, "which are all underground, hewn out of the live rock. The doors are cut out of immense blocks of stones, and are still standing and actually working on their hinges and used by the natives."

FROM THE COUNTRY OF THE GERGESENES TO CAPERNAUM.

Surrounded by a crowd,	Luke viii, 40; Mark v, 21.
Feast at Matthew's house,	Mark xv, 22; Luke v, 29-39.
Heals a woman with issue of blood and raises Jairus's daughter,	Matt. ix, 10-26; Mark v, 22-43; Luke viii, 41-56.
Heals two blind men and a dumb demoniac,	Matt. ix, 27-34.

The multitude had not forgotten the great Teacher nor had they departed to their homes. The crowd are present to receive him as he returns from the eastern coast.

It is generally believed that at this time Matthew gave the Lord a feast at his home. It was probably very like what we see now in Palestine. Dr. Geikie describes one he attended at Hebron thus: "A huge round tray of tinned copper, set on a low wooden stool, served for table, and to support a smaller, but still large tray, set in the middle of it, heaped up with a mound of boiled rice, soaked with melted butter, and abounding all through with small bits of meat. Besides this, which was the main preparation, there were smaller dishes of meat and vegetables. The guests squatted on the pieces of carpet in the middle of the room, their knees drawn up to their bodies, and, as at humbler entertainments, most of these dipped their hands into the dish for what they wanted, though a few used wooden spoons and plates of tinned copper, which, however, were not known in the days of Christ. When anyone had finished he rose and retired to the next room, to have his hands washed by water being poured over them, his empty place at the table being immediately filled up by some one still dinnerless."[1]

After the feast at Matthew's house—how long after we have no means of knowing—a ruler of the synagogue calls for the Lord to go and heal his little daughter lying at the point of death. On the way he meets the woman with the issue of blood and heals her. Returning from Jairus's house to his own home two blind men come to him and are given their sight. Later a dumb demoniac is brought to him and is healed.

[1] *New Testament Hours.*

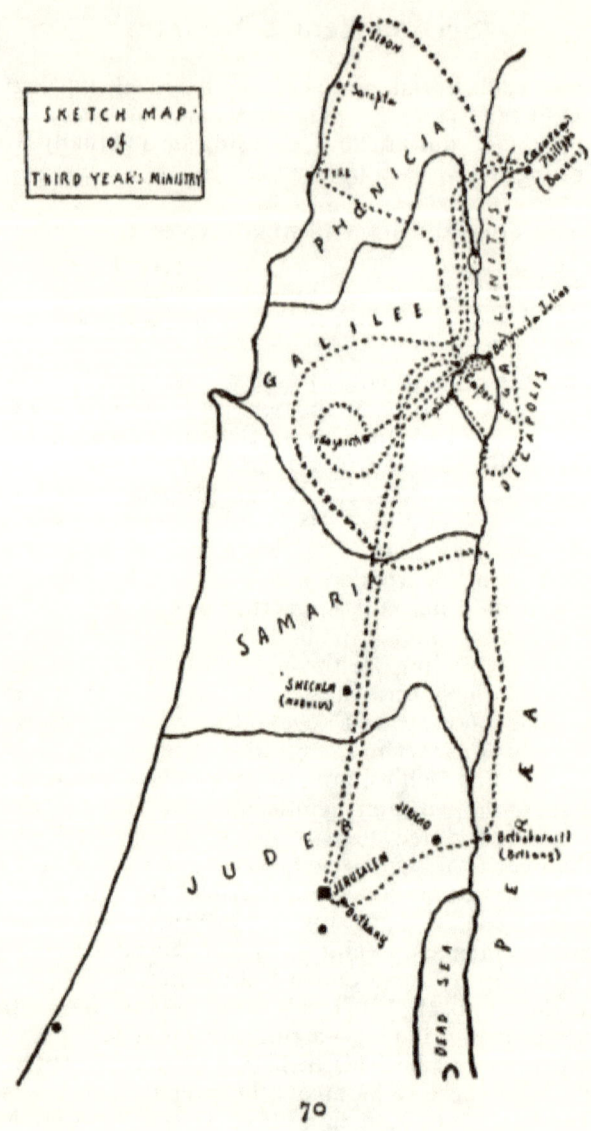

Third Year's Ministry

CHAPTER V.

Third Year's Ministry, January to December, A. D. 29.

ITINERARY ON MAP.—Capernaum—Nazareth and surrounding Towns—Capernaum—Across the Sea of Galilee to Plain of Butaiha—" Land of Gennesaret "—Capernaum—Coasts of Tyre and Sidon — Decapolis — Magdala — Capernaum — Bethsaida Julias—Capernaum—Jerusalem — Cæsarea Philippi — Through Galilee to Capernaum—Through Galilee, Samaria, Peræa to Bethany—Jerusalem.

FROM CAPERNAUM TO NAZARETH, THENCE TO SEVERAL CITIES AND VILLAGES IN THE SURROUNDING REGION.

Rejected the second time, ... Matt. xiii, 54-58 ; Mark vi, 1-6a.
Preaching tour, ... Mark ix, 35 ; Mark vi, 6b.
Commissions and sends out the twelve, . . Matt. ix, 36-38 ; x.
Hears of John's death, . . Matt. xiv, 1-12 ; Mark vi, 14-29 ; Luke ix, 7-9.

AS we follow the Lord to Nazareth, on this his second formal visit to that town since the beginning of his ministry, we cannot but be greatly impressed with the changes that have taken place since he was first harshly driven out by his fellow-townsmen. Then he was scarcely known beyond his own town. Now the whole country has heard of him, and great crowds from all parts of the country follow him. Yet his old acquaintances, and even his former friends, cannot believe that he is anything more than the son of the carpenter, and they are offended at him.

We may visit nearly all the surrounding territory and feel quite sure that we are walking in the footsteps of Christ when he "went about *all* the cities and villages."

His commission to and his sending out of his disciples made such a commotion that it seemed to the wicked Herod that John the Baptist had come to life. What sorrow must have filled the heart of Jesus when he learned that this faithful servant, the forerunner, was dead! John's death he doubtless received as prophetic of his own, though this was the most popular period of his ministry.

In His Footsteps

FROM NAZARETH AND SURROUNDING REGION TO CAPERNAUM, THENCE ACROSS THE SEA OF GALILEE TO PLAIN OF BUTAIHA, NEAR BETHSAIDA JULIAS.

Return of the twelve to Capernaum, . . . Mark vi, 30; Luke ix, 10a.
Across the Sea to Plain of Butaiha (El Batiha;) heals the sick and feeds five thousand men, besides women and children, Matt. xiv, 13-21; Mark vi, 31-44; Luke ix, 10b-17; John vi, 1-14.

After the return of the twelve to the Lord at Capernaum the crowds become so great, and their demands so taxing, that he invites his disciples to go apart to rest a while. They leave Capernaum in one of the fishing boats, crossing the upper end of the lake directly eastward to a small plain, which lies right on the shore near the old city of Bethsaida Julias.¹ But the people had seen the Lord and his disciples depart, and they ran afoot around the lake, arriving at the plain or "desert place" ahead of the boat. Seeing the multitude Jesus had pity on them. He healed many of their sick, and then, in the evening, fed them by means of a great miracle. We should not forget that the five loaves and two fishes which the Lord so wonderfully increased were furnished by a small boy. Boys and girls have much which the Lord can use for good if it is dedicated to him.

FROM PLAIN OF BUTAIHA TO "LAND OF GENNESARET," THENCE TO CAPERNAUM.

Jesus sends away the twelve, dismisses the multitude, and goes into a mountain to pray, Matt. xiv, 22, 23; Mark vi, 44-46; John vi, 15.
Jesus walks on the sea to the ship laboring in the storm, . Matt. xiv, 24-33; Mark vi, 47-52; John vi, 16-21a.
Arrives at the "land of Gennesaret," . . . Matt. xiv, 34-36; Mark vi, 53-56; John vi, 21b.

At Capernaum:

The bread of life, ... John vi, 22-71.
Discourse on eating with unwashen hands, . Matt. xv, 1-20; Mark vii, 1-23.

After such a laborious day as that on which the multitudes were fed it would seem that Jesus must needs have rest. But, no; he feels more the need of prayer. He sends away his disciples, dismisses the people, and goes into a mountain apart to pray. What mountain it was we do not know. But upon any one of those elevations surrounding the Sea of Galilee he would find retirement. No spot can seem more hallowed than where the Lord prayed.

¹ There was another Bethsaida on the west side of the Jordan near the lake.

Third Year's Ministry

But during the night a heavy storm arose, and the little boat with the disciples is almost swamped in the waves. But they cannot go down, for Jesus is watching them, "apart" though he is, and guarding them. He walks upon the waves, where we cannot follow him, except as we move in our boat toward the western coast. The disciples are greatly alarmed when they first see their Master, but Peter, recognizing him, walks on the water toward the Lord, who gets into the boat, and forthwith there is a great calm. They land somewhere on the plain of Gennesaret (Gennesareth), which lies just south of Capernaum.¹ The people are waiting for them. Many sick are healed, and then Jesus with the twelve goes to Capernaum.

At Capernaum Christ speaks about himself as the "bread of life." Some of his disciples are offended and forsake him, but the twelve cleave to him.

At that same time the Lord reproves the Pharisees for criticising his disciples because they ate with unwashed hands.

FROM CAPERNAUM INTO THE COASTS OF TYRE AND SIDON.

Heals the daughter of the Syrophenician woman, Matt. xv, 21-28; Mark vii, 24-30.

There is no data on which we may base an opinion as to the length of time Jesus was in Capernaum after his return from the feeding of the five thousand. It would seem that he did not stay long.

With the twelve he sets out on one of his longest trips and in a country unfamiliar to both him and us. The region in which are the cities of Tyre and Sidon lies northwest of the Sea of Galilee, bordering the coast of the Mediterranean. " Leaving Capernaum with his disciples, he took apparently a quiet track over the hills of Galilee to Tyre, thirty-five miles across the map, but necessarily a much longer road to travel." Sidon is twenty-five miles north of Tyre along the Mediterranean coast. It is not certain that Jesus actually entered either of these cities. If he did he found Tyre "still in its glory as a busy seaport. On the north was the Sidonian harbor, and on the south the Egyptian, each being about twelve acres in area. There are still remains which tell of its old busy days, though the doom prophesied has at last over-

---

¹ " The land of Gennesareth, which is identified with the marshy plain, *El Ghuweir*, which stretches for three miles along the shore of the lake in its northwest corner." Henderson, *Palestine*.

In His Footsteps

taken it (Ezek. xxvi–xxviii, 19). In excavating great heaps of shells have been turned over, from which the famous dye had been obtained, and broken lumps of glass that mark the site of its not less famous glassworks. It was a busy and heathen city when he passed by the sands of its sea coast."[1] Sidon was a still older city than Tyre. "In Homer's day it was famed for its silversmiths, and in that of Xerxes for its shipbuilders." On visiting the site of ancient Tyre we find it occupied by a town called Sur, containing five thousand inhabitants, about half of them being Mohammedans. Sidon,

MODERN TYRE.

now Saida. It has a population of fifteen thousand. There is an American mission there, with a boys' and girls' school.

While passing through this "heathen" territory a woman— a Canaanite by birth and a Greek by language—came and besought him to cure her afflicted daughter. Had no one else sought him, the woman's noble faith repaid him for his journey.

FROM THE COAST OF TYRE AND SIDON TO THE REGION KNOWN AS DECAPOLIS.

Heals many, ... Matt. xv, 29-31; Mark vii, 31-37.
Feeds four thousand, ... Matt. xv, 32-38; Mark viii, 1-9.

Decapolis was the name given to ten cities lying on the eastern and southern shores of the Sea of Galilee. With one

---

[1] Henderson, *Palestine*.

Third Year's Ministry

exception these ten cities lay on the eastern side of the Jordan. The Lord, after passing north through the region of Sidon, would probably turn southeast and cross the Jordan, following the river southward until he came "unto the Sea of Galilee through the midst of the coasts of Decapolis." The route is not a particularly desirable one save for the fine mountain scenery of eastern Phœnicia and Upper Galilee. On this trip we get our best view of Mount Hermon, to which we shall make another journey very soon.

Here, as elsewhere, though the Lord had visited it but once before, when he healed the demoniacs at Gersa, great crowds are drawn to him, and he heals many diseases.

For three days the people surround him, and at their close he feeds four thousand "with seven loaves and a few fishes." Some think this miracle was performed on the same spot as that for the five thousand, but it seems more reasonable to believe, as most of these cities lay toward the southern shore of Galilee, that it occurred in that neighborhood.

FROM DECAPOLIS TO MAGDALA (MAGADAN), THENCE TO CAPERNAUM.

To Magdala (Revised Version, Magadan), . . Matt. xv, 39; Mark viii, 10.
At Capernaum, Pharisees and Sadducees
   demand a sign, ... Matt. xvi, 1-4; Mark viii, 11, 12.

There has been much discussion on the location of Magdala, or Magadan, as the Revised Version has it. Mark does not mention Magadan, but says that Christ and his disciples, after entering into a boat, "came into the parts of Dalmanutha." We cannot enter into the discussion, but conclude to follow those who identify Magdala, or Magadan, with El Mejdel, "a miserable village on the south side of the plain of Gennesaret, near the lake." Probably the Dalmanutha of Mark was so near Magdala that the latter was sometimes called by the other name.[1]

From Magdala the Lord probably went to Capernaum, and there met the Pharisees and Sadducees, who have come demanding a sign from heaven as to his claim to be the Messiah. Over this ground we have already gone many times.

---

[1] "Just before reaching Mejdel we crossed a little open valley, with a few cornfields and gardens straggling among the ruins of a village, and some large and more ancient foundations by several copious fountains, probably identified with Dalmanutha."—*Tristram*.

In His Footsteps

FROM CAPERNAUM TO BETHSAIDA.

On the way,	Matt. xvi, 5-12; Mark viii, 13-21.
Heals a blind man at Bethsaida,	Mark viii, 22-26.

After the Pharisees and Sadducees had made their demand that Jesus give them a "sign from heaven," it is recorded that the Lord "sighed deeply in his spirit," grieved beyond expression that they would not receive the signs he had already given them of the truth he had taught and preached. He now determines to turn away from them, for he knows their hearts are too hardened to be convinced. With his disciples he crosses the upper part of the lake in a boat. While going over, observing that the disciples had not provided themselves with food, he warns them of the leaven of the Pharisees. They land at a familiar place, the plain of Butaiha, where the five thousand had been fed. From there they go up to Bethsaida Julias, where a blind man is healed.

Bethsaida Julias lies three quarters of a mile from the lake, on the slope of a hill. It is now, as we find it, a heap of ruins. It was the birthplace of Peter, John, and Philip, and was rebuilt by Herod's son and named Julias in honor of the daughter of Augustus, Emperor of Rome.

FROM BETHSAIDA JULIAS TO CAPERNAUM, THENCE TO JERUSALEM.[1]

The Lord meets his brethren at Capernaum,	John vii, 2-9.
Goes to Jerusalem secretly,	John vii, 10.

At Jerusalem:

Encounter with the Jews,	John vii, 11-52.
Visit to Mount of Olives,	John viii, 1.
Return to the temple,	John viii, 2-58.
Leaves the temple to escape stoning,	John viii, 59.
Heals a blind man,	John ix.
The good shepherd,	John x, 1-21.

If the Lord went from Bethsaida Julias to Jerusalem to attend the feast of the tabernacles, it would be natural for him to go by way of Capernaum, as that place is not more

---

[1] At this point we meet one of the greatest difficulties in harmonizing the gospel narrative. Most writers think that from Bethsaida Julias Jesus went with the twelve north to Cæsarea Philippi, and then to the scene of the transfiguration; that afterward he went to Jerusalem to attend the feast of tabernacles which took place in October. Two months later occurred the feast of dedication, which Jesus also attended. Some believe the Lord did not return to Galilee in the interval between the two feasts. The objections to the above are, (1) the statement of John that "Jesus would not walk in Jewry because the Jews sought to kill him;" (2) the statement of Matthew, Mark, and Luke of another departure of the Lord from Galilee after the one mentioned by John to the feast of

Third Year's Ministry

than an hour's walk around the shore from Bethsaida Julias. The interview with his brethren was probably at Capernaum.

The Lord's brethren were anxious for him to go to Jerusalem and declare himself openly as the Messiah. They believed that the rulers would accept his claims. "Had Jesus been such a Messiah as they supposed was to come their advice was good. It is plain that they did not in any true sense believe on him, but in a spirit of purely worldly wisdom attempted to guide him in his conduct. Their advice was in its nature a temptation like that of the devil; a temptation to reveal himself before the time and in a presumptuous way."¹ He waits in Capernaum a few days, and then sets off as quietly as possible to avoid the crowd. "The object of his delay was to avoid going with the great Galilean caravan, which entered the holy city with public rejoicings. He would be

A BLIND BEGGAR.

recognized at once, and the multitude, in the excitement of the time, might again try to force him into political action.

---

tabernacles (Matt. xix, 1; Mark x, 1; Luke ix, 51). It seems clear, therefore, that Jesus must have returned to Galilee after the feast of tabernacles in October, and the most reasonable conclusion, in view of all the facts, is that that return took place within the two months between the two feasts. Andrews's summary of the whole question is very able, and his arrangement of events is provisionally adopted until more light is thrown on this very difficult problem of Gospel harmony.
¹ Andrews, *The Life of Our Lord*.

In His Footsteps

Publicity and popular enthusiasm would have drawn the attention of those in power, and this he at present earnestly wished to avoid. His work was not to be rashly broken off by any imprudent act, for he needed all the opportunities that remained to devote himself to the twelve and to his other followers. He could go up a few days later, and thus avoid the caravan. The feast lasted seven days, closing with the eighth as the greatest, and thus, even if he started later, he could mingle with the multitudes and find out how men felt toward him and his work, and proclaim the new kingdom as he saw fit. The danger would be averted, and his great end better served. It was more in keeping with his spirit to avoid all appearance of courting popularity and to deliver his great message of love in stillness, leaving its reception to its own charms and to the lowly humility, self-denial, and greatness with which it was delivered."[1]

THE WATERS OF MEROM.

With what sorrow must he have entered his Father's house on this occasion. It is a time of joy for others, yet he must come as a criminal hiding from justice. "The feast of tabernacles (or ingathering) was intended to commemorate the passage of the Israelites through the wilderness, and was celebrated with such universal joy that both Josephus and Philo call it 'the holiest and greatest feast,' and it was known among the Jews as '*the feast*' preeminently. It was kept for seven consecutive days, from the 15th to the 21st of Tisri, and the eighth was celebrated by a holy convocation. During the seven days the Jews celebrated their desert wanderings, lived in booths made of thickly foliaged boughs of olive and palm and pine and myrtle. During the week of festivities all the courses of priests were employed in turn; seventy bullocks were offered in sacrifice for the seventy nations of the world;

---
[1] Geikie, *Life of Christ*.

Third Year's Ministry

the law was daily read, and on each day the temple trumpets sounded twenty-one times an inspiring and triumphant blast. The joy of the occasion was deepened by the fact that the feast followed but four days after the ceremonies of the great day of atonement, in which a solemn expiation was made for the sins of the people."[1]

As soon as the Lord entered the temple he was recognized and attacked. He is accused of having a devil. Nicodemus, who came to him by night, a member of the Sanhedrin, endeavors to have justice done, but he is himself charged with being in league with Jesus. The spirit of the Jews is no-

CÆSAREA PHILIPPI.

where so well shown as in the efforts of the Pharisees to persuade the blind man that he had not been cured.

Then are spoken those precious words which have comforted so many burdened hearts and have been the inspiration of childhood: "I am the good shepherd; the good shepherd layeth down his life for the sheep."[2]

---

[1] Farrar, *Life of Christ*.
[2] "When the thief and the robber come (and come they do), the faithful shepherd has often to put his life in his hand to defend his flock. I have known more than one case in which he had literally to lay it down in the contest."—*Thomson*.

In His Footsteps

FROM JERUSALEM TO THE REGION OF CÆSAREA PHILIPPI.

Talks by the way, . . Matt. xvi, 13-28; Mark viii, 27-ix, 1; Luke ix, 18-27.
The transfiguration, . . Matt. xvii, 1-9; Mark ix, 2-10; Luke ix, 28-36.
Discourse on the coming of Elias, . . Matt. xvii, 10-13; Mark ix, 11-13.
The lunatic boy, . . . Matt. vii, 14-21; Mark ix, 14-29; Luke ix, 37-43.

We have before us one of our longest continuous trips, about one hundred and twenty miles. The only part of the route with which we are unfamiliar is that lying between the Sea of Galilee and Cæsarea Philippi, a stretch of country between thirty-five and forty miles in length. We pass Chorazin (Kerazeh) on our right, a heap of ruins, reminding us of our Lord's prophecy (Matt. xi, 21), skirt the mountains of Safed on the left and reach Lake Merom, now known as Lake Huleh. It is only about fifteen feet deep, and "abounds in waterfowl, including pelicans and wild duck, but swamps render it difficult or impossible of access on the north side, on which rises a dense jungle of papyrus." North of the lake is a plain some five miles in width. Toward the east the bed of the valley forms a swamp in which the buffaloes belonging to the Bedouins wallow. We turn toward the northeast, crossing the river near Dan, and are in sight of the beautifully situated Banias (Cæsarea Philippi). This was in ancient times the Greek Baneas. It was enlarged by Herod's son Philip, and given the name Cæsarea, to which Philippi was afterward added. It is one thousand one hundred and fifty feet above sea level, situated in a nook of Mount Hermon.

A LITTLE CHILD OF PALESTINE.

Into this vicinity came our Lord with the twelve, and somewhere on this very mountain of Hermon he was transfigured. What a change from the scene of the temple in Jerusalem, with the Pharisees plotting to kill him! How often the rejected of men is the accepted of God!

Descending from the mountain the Lord finds his waiting

Third Year's Ministry

disciples, helpless to heal an afflicted child. He teaches them the needed lesson of faith, and casts out the evil spirit.

FROM CÆSAREA PHILIPPI THROUGH GALILEE TO CAPERNAUM.

On the way,	Matt. xvii, 22, 23 ; Luke ix, 43-45.
At Capernaum : The tribute money,	Matt. xvii, 24-27.
A little child in the midst,	Mark ix, 33-50 ; Luke ix, 4-50.

We return southward through Galilee to Capernaum. On the way the Lord speaks to his disciples of his approaching death, but they do not understand him.

At Capernaum Peter comes saying that the Master is expected to pay the temple tax. "The exact time for payment had passed while Christ had been away from Capernaum. As if to show that not even the most insignificant matter that concerned his disciples escaped his notice, even when not bodily present with them, Peter no sooner appeared than his errand was anticipated."[1]

The twelve had been trying to settle the remarkable question who was the greatest among them. Jesus sets a little child before them and tells them that not the largest in size, nor the most learned, nor those who thought they possessed special privileges were the greatest in the kingdom, but those without worldly ambition, the teachable and the trustful; such, indeed, as had the spirit of the little child now before them.

FROM CAPERNAUM THROUGH GALILEE, SAMARIA, AND PERÆA TO BETHANY.

Final departure from Galilee,	Matt. xix, 1 ; Mark x, 1 ; Luke ix, 51.
In Samaria,	Luke ix, 52-56.

In Peræa. Incidents by the way:

The seventy sent in advance,	Matt. ix, 20-24 ; Luke x, 1-16.
Jesus follows,	Mark x, 1.
Return of the seventy,	Matt. xi, 25-30 ; Luke x, 17-24.
The Good Samaritan,	Luke x, 25-37.
Teaching to pray,	Luke xi, 1-13.
Healing the blind and dumb,	Matt. xii, 22, 23 ; Luke xi, 14.
Concerning the Pharisees,	Matt. xii, 24-45 ; Mark iii, 22-30.
Feast at a Pharisee's house and parable of the rich fool,	Luke xi, 3-54-xii.
Parable of the fig tree,	Luke xiii, 2-9.
Healing of an infirm woman on the Sabbath,	Luke xiii, 10-17.
Parables of mustard seed and leaven,	Luke xiii, 18-21.
"Strive to enter in"—warning against Herod,	Luke xiii, 22-35.
At Bethany,	Luke x, 22-35.

We are passing through Galilee for the last time previous to the crucifixion, as this journey marks the Lord's final departure from that province.

---
[1] Geikie, *Life of Christ*

In His Footsteps

The Lord sends James and John in advance to provide entertainment for the company at one of the Samaritan villages, but the bigoted people will not allow the party to stay in their village because they are going toward Jerusalem. John and James want to call down fire from heaven, but the Lord severely rebukes them.

They then turn toward the eastern side of the Jordan to a province called Peræa.[1] The Lord sends the seventy before him to announce his coming, and thus prepare the people among whom he has not yet labored for his teaching. There were many towns in Peræa when Jesus passed through it;

BETHANY.

there is scarcely anything but ruins now. We have already passed through the territory in following our Lord to his baptism.

Jesus evidently did not stay long in one place, but continued moving toward the south, teaching and healing. One day he is at a feast in a Pharisee's house, the next he is healing some poor creature who has found help nowhere else.

Finally he crosses the Jordan westward, probably near Bethabara, where he was baptized, and reaches Bethany, the home of Martha and Mary, where he finds a welcome awaiting him. Bethany is now known as El-Azariyeh. It lies two miles east of the capital on the Jerusalem and Jericho road,

---

[1] "Peræa is mentioned in the gospels (Matt. iv, 25) under the term, 'beyond Jordan,' Πέραν τοῦ Ἰορδάνου; in Mark x, 1, translated 'the farther side of Jordan.'"—*Andrews.*

"In the time of Christ it was fertile and populous and inhabited by a mixed population, partly Roman, partly Jewish."—*Lyman Abbott.*

Third Year's Ministry

nestling "in a sheltered nook at the point where the road over the summit descends into the southern one. There is no question as to its identity."[1] It is endeared to us because it afforded at least one place where the Son of man might lay his head. We are shown the "tomb of Lazarus" and the site of the house of Mary and Martha.

FROM BETHANY TO JERUSALEM.[2]

At the feast of dedication, ... John x, 22, 23.
Controversy with the Jews, ... John x, 24-39.

We pass around the Mount of Olives, entering Jerusalem, not as formerly by the Damascus Gate, but by one of the gates on the east. Jesus entered the city at this time to attend the feast of dedication. "The festival of dedication was instituted by Judas Maccabeus to commemorate the purification of the temple and the renewal of the temple worship after the three years of profanation by Antiochus Epiphanes. It was held during eight days, commencing on the 25th day of the month Kisler, which began with the new moon of December. It was celebrated by the Jews, not at Jerusalem alone, like the great festivals of the law, but at home, throughout the whole country, by the festive illumination of their dwellings."[3]

While the Lord was walking on the eastern side of the temple in Solomon's porch—so called because it was built of materials which had formed part of the ancient temple—he is met by the Jews who want a plain statement as to his Messiahship. The Lord's reply so angers them that they try to kill him.

---
[1] Henderson, *Palestine*.
[2] We cannot be sure of any of these events during these "last days," but Andrews is followed throughout as the most satisfactory guide.
[3] Robinson.

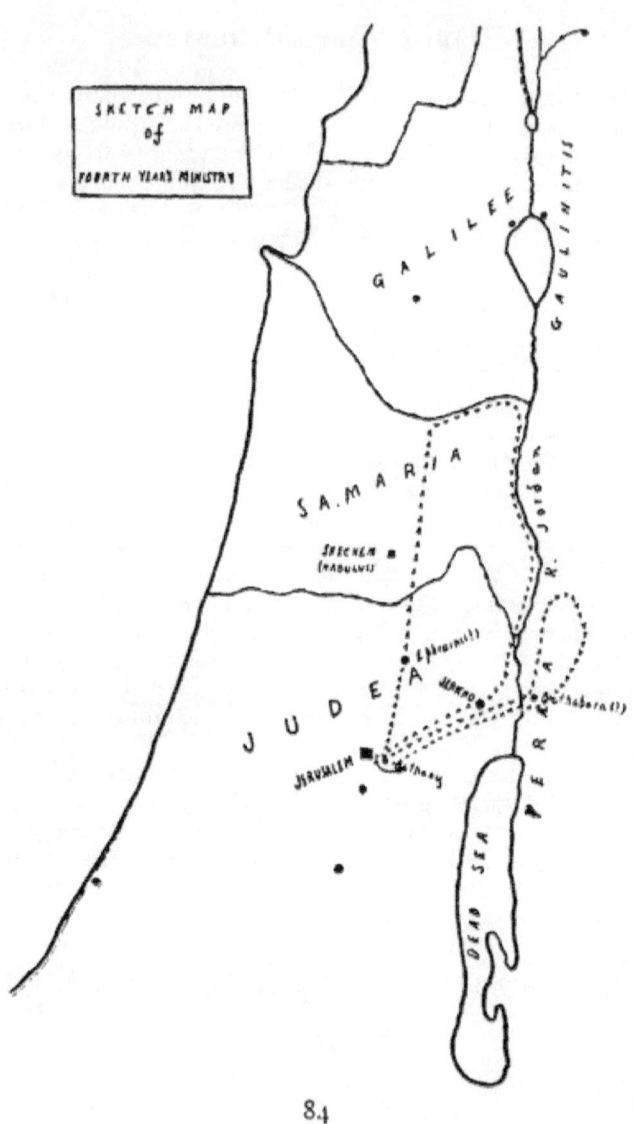

Fourth Year's Ministry

CHAPTER VI.

Fourth Year's Ministry, January to April 2, A. D. 30.

ITINERARY ON MAP. — Jerusalem — Peræa through Bethabara (Bethany) — Bethany (near Jerusalem) — Ephraim — Jericho by way of the border of Samaria and Galilee and the Jordan valley — Bethany.

FROM JERUSALEM TO PERÆA THROUGH BETHABARA (BETHANY).

Departure from Jerusalem,	John x, 40.
Many come to him at Bethabara,	John x, 41, 42.
Attends a feast at a Pharisee's house, heals a dropsical man, gives advice in choosing one's place, and delivers parable of great supper,	Luke xiv, 1-24.
The test of discipleship,	Luke xiv, 25-35.
Parables of lost sheep, lost piece of silver, prodigal son, and unjust steward,	Luke xv ; xvi, 1-13.
Pharisees reproved,	Luke xvi, 14-18.
Parables of rich man and Lazarus,	Luke xvi, 19-31.
Advice to disciples,	Luke xvii, 1-10.

ACCORDING to John, Jesus, immediately after the attack upon him at the feast of dedication, "went away again beyond Jordan into the place where John was at the first baptizing." The scene of John's labors (Bethabara or Bethany—not the Bethany of Mary and Martha, of course) we have already located on the Jordan, directly east of Jericho, on the opposite side of the river. Going down from Jerusalem to Jericho we realize why the unfortunate Jew was robbed on this same road. It is extremely rugged and dangerous, affording many hiding places for thieves. We skirt the Mount of Olives and pass Bethany on our right toward the southeast. Ascending a hill we come to the "stone of rest," said to be the place where Martha and Mary met Jesus when he was on his way to Bethany to raise Lazarus from the dead. We pass several ruins, cross several brooks, mountains, valleys, and plains, and finally reach Jericho, which we do not now visit, but hasten on to the ford of Jordan, some five miles beyond Jericho. This has been a gathering place for many centuries for Christians who came to be bap-

In His Footsteps

tized in the waters of Jordan. In the sixth century Antoninus records "that both banks were paved with marble, that a wooden cross rose in the middle of the stream, and that, after the water had been blessed by the priest, the pilgrims entered it, each wearing a linen garment, which was carefully preserved afterward in order to be used as a winding-sheet."[1]

Arriving at Bethabara Jesus was visited by large companies of people, and "many believed on him." From Bethabara he probably went to several other places in Peræa. The time from the feast of dedication in December to the passover, a period of about four months, was occupied with this ministry on the eastern shore of the Jordan, the visit to Bethany near Jerusalem, the stay in Ephraim, and the journey from Ephraim back to Bethany by way of Jericho. We may reasonably suppose that the ministry in Peræa did not occupy more than two months.

"THE BLOODY WAY"—ON THE ROAD FROM JERUSALEM TO JERICHO.

From the scene of John's baptism we go with Luke to the other points in Peræa. The Lord is invited to the home of a prominent Pharisee, and while there on a Sabbath heals a man of dropsy, advises his disciples not to choose the most conspicuous places, and gives the parable of the great supper. How appropriate such words at that time. They had just partaken of a feast, and possibly some of them had secretly wished for conspicuous seats. They had all responded gladly to the invitation of this prominent Pharisee to eat of the good things which had been provided. Would they all respond as heartily to the invitation of their Father in heaven to eat of the good things of his table? Then comes the test of discipleship—and a close and searching

[1] Baedeker, *Palestine and Syria*.

Fourth Year's Ministry

test it is—the parables of the lost sheep, the lost piece of money, the prodigal son, and the unjust steward. These parables are very much more interesting, because much clearer, since we have seen the country in which the customs and life referred to are familiar even to this day.

"The bitter poverty of the East would itself account for the wild eagerness of the search after a trifling coin; but there were other impulses. At Bethlehem the women wear a row of coins over their forehead, and their sisters of Nazareth wear strings of them at each side of the face. At both places these constitute, as a rule, the whole wealth of their possessor, and have been inherited as an heirloom from previous owners, a mother, grandmother, or even some one farther back. That the string should break and let one of the little store, thus sacred, be lost, might well make the unfortunate sufferer not only light her poor lamp but sweep the floor over in the hope of finding the precious sixpence or shilling."[1]

WOMAN WITH HEADDRESS OF COINS.

The food of the swine which the poor prodigal was at last forced to eat we often see. It is the fruit of the carob tree, which "rises to a height of from twenty to thirty feet, looking like a huge apple tree, and attracting the eye at once by its abundant foliage of dark glossy evergreen leaves." Dr. Geikie says that immense quantities of the carob pods are sold in England for horse fodder. They can be seen at many fruit stands in our largest American cities.

The Lord again reproves the Pharisees; in this instance

[1] Geikie, *New Testament Hours.*

for their love of money and their indifference to the condition of the poor. Even now, in the East, we are brought almost daily into contact with those who try to impress us with their high social position by wearing gaudy colors.

FROM PERÆA TO BETHANY (NEAR JERUSALEM).

After two days Jesus starts for Bethany,	John xi, 1-6.
Conversation about Lazarus on the way,	John xi, 7-16.
Meeting with Martha and Mary outside Bethany,	John xi, 17-38.
At the grave of Lazarus,	John xi, 39-44.
The Pharisees plot against Jesus,	John xi, 45-53.

Jesus probably took the road past Jericho toward Jerusalem, the same on which we journeyed following him to Bethabara. The sisters meet the Lord just before he reaches Bethany, and tell him of all that is in their hearts. Then Jesus goes with them into the village to the place where Lazarus was buried.

The effect of the miracle was so great that the Lord's enemies in Jerusalem are resolved to take his life.

FROM BETHANY TO EPHRAIM.

In retirement there,	John xi, 54, 55
Anxiously sought for by his enemies in Jerusalem,	John xi, 56, 57.

Here we meet with another of the difficulties of biblical geography. We do not know where Ephraim was. The best authorities on the geography of the Bible, Porter, Lange, Ellicott, Conder, Tristram, Henderson, and George Adam Smith, believe it was the village now known as Taiyebeh, some fifteen miles almost directly north of Jerusalem. We shall accept this conclusion, in want of more reliable data, and journey thither. We turn from Bethany, toward the north, avoiding Jerusalem, pass through Anata (the ancient Anathoth, Jeremiah's birthplace), Jeba or Gebah, then down through the pass and village of Mikhmash, the village of Der Divan, "loftily situated and inclosed by mountains." Then directly north to Taiyebeh (Ephraim). "It is a village perched on a conspicuous eminence and with an extensive view."

The Lord's reason for going to Ephraim was clearly to escape the malice of his enemies in Jerusalem, for his time had not yet come. "He was spending the few days that remained to him, not amid crowds, nor renewing in some scattered villages the labors of his early ministry, but in the society of

Fourth Year's Ministry

his disciples, teaching them such truths as they could receive, and preparing them for their labors after he should himself be taken from them. Doubtless, also, this period gave him many desired opportunities of solitary communion with his father."[1]

FROM EPHRAIM NORTH TO THE BORDER OF SAMARIA AND GALILEE, THENCE EAST TO THE JORDAN, FOLLOWING THE WESTERN SHORE SOUTH TO JERICHO.

Ten lepers cleansed on border of Samaria, . . . Luke xvii, 11-19.
Talks on the way to Jericho: The coming kingdom, . . Luke xvii, 20-37.
Parables of unjust judge and Pharisee and publican, . . Luke xviii, 1-14.
Discourse on divorce, ... Matt. xix, 3-12; Mark x, 2-12.
Children blessed, . . Matt. xix, 13-15; Mark x, 13-16; Luke xviii, 15-17.
The rich young ruler, . Matt. xix, 16-30; Mark x, 17-31; Luke xviii, 18-30.
Laborers in the vineyard. . . . . Matt. xx, 1-16.
Jesus foretells his death, Matt. xx, 17-19; Mark x, 32-34; Luke xviii, 31-34.
John and James want position, . . . Matt. xx, 20-28; Mark x, 35-45.
Near Jericho: Blind healed, Matt. xx, 29-34; Mark x, 46-52; Luke xviii, 35-43.
In Jericho: Interview with Zaccheus, ... Luke xix, 1-10.
Parable of the pounds, ... Luke xix, 11-28.

Luke clearly states that the healing of the ten lepers occurred while Jesus and his disciples were passing "through

LEPERS BEGGING BY THE WAYSIDE.

the midst of Samaria and Galilee" (Luke xvii, 11). The word translated "midst" would better be rendered "between." Evidently the Lord went north to the border between Samaria and Galilee, then turned east to the Jordan. We do not know why he chose this route, but probably to join the cara-

---
[1] Andrews, *The Life of Our Lord.*

In His Footsteps

van coming down from Galilee and the north to attend the passover.

The Lord's few weeks of retirement are ended, and he is now to enter Jerusalem, not as one afraid of his life, but boldly and with all publicity. He would probably choose the west bank of the river and proceed with the horde of pilgrims, meeting the crowds from the east side of the river at Jericho. Somewhere on the way he speaks of the approaching kingdom of which he is king, gives the parables of the unjust judge and the Pharisee and publican. He speaks about marriage, blesses little children, tells the rich young man what he must do if he would be perfect, gives the parable of the laborers in the vineyard, foretells his death, and, finally, tells James and John, and their mother Salome, what conditions are necessary for position in his kingdom.

Near Jericho the blind men were healed.[1] Going into the city he met Zaccheus, and probably lodged at his house over night. Somewhere in the city or near it he gave the parable of the pounds. When the Lord visited Jericho it was "probably among Judean cities second only to Jerusalem." In our Lord's day it was both beautiful and wealthy. It was the home of large numbers of priests and Levites, who could be seen almost any hour of the day on the road between Jerusalem and Jericho. Its glory has all departed. It now "consists of a group of squalid hovels inhabited by about three hundred souls." As we enter we are surrounded by the villagers, who declare their desire to dance for our pleasure (and for *backsheesh*). But it would hardly do to show money, as thieves are plentiful in Jericho. The site of the "house of Zaccheus" and other relics are pointed out. The fruits and flowers of the region are very interesting. The famous "rose of Jericho" is not a rose, neither is it found at Jericho, but farther south on the banks of the Dead Sea.

FROM JERICHO TO BETHANY.

Arrival at Bethany, ... John xii, 1.
Anointing by Mary, . . Matt. xxvi, 6-13; Mark xiv, 3-9; John xii, 2-11.

Our present trip toward Jerusalem is of pathetic interest, as it is the last long journey we shall take with Jesus before the crucifixion. He is going up to Jerusalem to die.

---
[1] For a full discussion of the questions when and where the blind men were healed, see Andrews, *The Life of Our Lord*, pp. 416-418.

Fourth Year's Ministry

It was but natural that just before his great struggle, which ended only with his life, the Lord should turn toward Bethany to a home that was always open and always dear to him.

He arrives on Friday. A supper is made for him, and Mary, forgetting all else in her affection for her Lord, pours upon his head and feet the most precious thing she had, the Eastern spikenard, and then wipes his feet with her hair. A greater tribute of love could not have been shown. The alabaster vase was very precious in itself, but that Mary broke. "To anoint the feet was a supreme expression of honor, and still more so when the ointment used was not the common manufacture, but the hugely dear ointment brought from distant Eastern countries."

The act doubtless surprised all the disciples who were not used to seeing such costly articles, but only Judas, whose covetousness and avarice were too great to be restrained, protests openly.

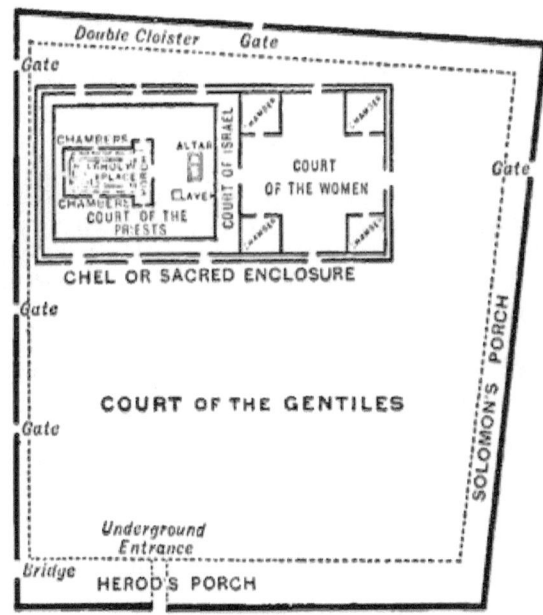

PLAN OF HEROD'S TEMPLE.

CHAPTER VII.

Passion Week.[1]

Sunday, April 2, A. D. 30.

FROM BETHANY TO JERUSALEM—RETURN TO BETHANY.

On the way, Matt. xxi, 1-11; Mark xi, 1-10; Luke xix, 29-40; John xii, 12-19.
Weeping over the city, ... Luke xix, 41-44.
In the temple. . . . . Mark xi, 11a.
Return to Bethany, ... Mark xi, 11b.

IT is generally believed that Jesus spent Friday night, Saturday, and Saturday night at Bethany. On Sunday, the first day of the week, he made his triumphal entry into Jerusalem. It is well known that all the friends of Jesus had anxiously awaited such a moment. They had openly pressed him to declare himself and thus inaugurate his glorious reign as the King of Israel. The Lord had patiently sought to turn their minds away from a worldly kingdom and worldly methods of advancing it. Up to this time he had resisted everything like display. Now, however, he will go into Jerusalem as a king. But how unlike the kings of the earth! Instead of the spears are palm branches; instead of the blare of trumpets, the voice of psalms; instead of the warlike horse, a beast which symbolizes peace and humility.

The route from Bethany to Jerusalem was over the usual road that wound across the Mount of Olives. Following our Lord during these last days, we mark more particularly each step of the way. There is nothing of special interest after leaving Bethany until we reach the Mount of Olives. This is a "long ridge of chalky limestone" just east of Jerusalem and parallel to it, separated from the city by the valley of the Kidron. This ridge, popularly known as the Mount of Olives, is really made up of three eminences; the northern one known as Mount Scopus, the southern as the Mount of Offense. The

---

[1] The rubric of Catholic churches makes passion week preceding that of the crucifixion. Protestant usage prefers the historical to the conventional order.

Passion Week

middle eminence is the distinctive Mount of Olives. These divisions we must always keep in mind as we follow our Lord's footsteps from day to day during this eventful week. The central mountain, which we have already marked as the Mount of Olives proper, has three points or projections; the northernmost being called Viri Galilæi, and is two thousand seven hundred and twenty-three feet above sea level, and nearly three hundred feet above the temple. The middle one now contains a Mohammedan village of a dozen homes called Et Tor. The third or southern projection is "inclosed and in possession of the Roman Catholics, who have here two churches and a convent." Of the Mount of Olives proper "the slopes are cultivated, but the vegetation is not

BETHANY.   OLIVET.   JERUSALEM.

luxuriant. The principal trees are the olive, fig, and carob, and here and there a few apricot, almond, terebinth, and hawthorn trees. The paths are stony and the afternoon sun very hot."[1]

Our road from Bethany runs "between the Mount of Offense and the Mount of Olives (proper), but there is another more direct running over the central summit." Our Lord probably chose the regular road. He sent his disciples ahead to Bethphage, a village or neighborhood somewhere on the road between Bethany and Mount of Olives, but whose site is now unknown, to secure the beast on which he is to make his advent into the city. Then, with a great company following, the Lord moves on to Jerusalem. "Two vast streams of

---

[1] Baedeker, *Palestine and Syria*.

In His Footsteps

people met on that day. The one poured out from the city, and, as they came through the garden whose clusters of palm rose on the southeastern corner of Olivet, they cut down the long branches, as was their wont at the feast of tabernacles, and moved upward toward Bethany with loud shouts of welcome. From Bethany streamed forth the crowds who had assembled there the previous night. The two streams met midway. Half of the vast mass, turning round, preceded, the other half followed. Gradually the long procession swept up over the ridge where first begins ' the descent of the Mount of Olives' toward Jerusalem."[1]

After crossing the valley of the Kidron, now called Wady Sitti Maryam (Valley of St. Mary), the Lord went to the temple, looked about him for a time, and then returned to Bethany for the night.

Monday, April 3.

FROM BETHANY TO JERUSALEM—RETURN TO BETHANY.

The fig tree condemned, ... Matt. xxi, 18, 19; Mark xi, 12–14.
The temple purified, . Matt. xxi, 12, 13; Mark xi, 15–17; Luke xix, 45, 46.
Blind and lame healed, ... Matt. xxi, 14; Luke xix, 47, 48.
Priests and the scribes enraged, . . . Matt. xxi, 15, 16; Mark xi, 18.
Return to Bethany in the evening, . . . Matt. xxi, 17; Mark xi, 19.

There are many questions of chronology and harmony which we cannot pause to discuss. Jesus passing out of Bethany early on Monday morning, hungry, after perhaps a night of earnest prayer, sees a fig tree with its leaves so forward as to indicate ripened fruit. With his disciples he turns toward it, but finds nothing but leaves. That fig tree, with its fair show of fruit, represented the Jewish nation; Jesus therefore condemned it. In other words, he pronounced it what in reality it was, a hypocritical cumberer of the ground. "That our Lord should have cursed the fig tree on which there were leaves but no fruit is explained when we remember that the fruit appears before the leaves, and that in a tree so out of the common in its development those round him would expect that fruit would be also present, though it was not yet the season for it."[2]

Proceeding to the temple the Lord does not merely look about him, as on the previous day, but as in the beginning of his ministry, so now at its close, cleanses his Father's house

---
[1] Stanley, *Sinai and Palestine*.   [2] Geikie, *New Testament Hours*.

Passion Week

of its pollutions. Of course they would return again, but Jesus will do his duty nevertheless.

At the close of the day we return again with Jesus to Bethany.

Tuesday, April 4.

FROM BETHANY TO JERUSALEM—RETURN TO BETHANY.

On the way: Finds fig tree withered, lesson on
  faith, ... Matt. xxi, 20-22; Mark xi, 20-25.
In the temple: Christ's authority
  challenged, ... Matt. xxi, 23-27; Mark xi, 27-33; Luke xx, 1-8.
He answers in parables, . Matt. xxi, 28-xxii, 14; Mark xii, 1, 2; Luke xx, 9-19.
Three questions by Pharisees,
  Sadducees, and a lawyer, Matt. xxii, 15-40; Mark xii, 13-34, Luke xx, 20-40.
Christ's unanswered question, Matt. xxii, 41-46; Mark xii, 35-37; Luke xx, 41-44.
Hypocrites revealed and denounced, Matt. xxiii; Mark xii, 38-40; Luke xx, 45-47.
Jesus beside the treasury, ... Mark xii, 41-44; Luke xxi, 1-4.
Jesus and the Greeks, ... John xii, 20-36.
Going out of the temple: Conversation regarding
  destruction of temple, . . Matt. xxiv, 1, 2; Mark xiii, 1, 2; Luke xxi, 5, 6.
On Mount of Olives: Conversation regarding destruction of Jerusalem
  and the end of the world; parables of the fig tree, the virgins, and
  the talents, . Matt. xxiv, 3-51; xxv; xxvi, 1, 2; Mark xiii; Luke xxi, 5-38.
Return to Bethany, ... Mark xi, 19; Luke xxi, 37.
Judas counsels with Christ's
  enemies, . Matt. xxvi, 3-5; 14-16; Mark xiv, 1, 2; 10, 11; Luke xxii, 1-6.

Passing over the road from Bethany to Jerusalem, it is observed that the fig tree has withered away. From that the Lord draws a valuable lesson on faith.

Arriving at the temple, the Pharisees seek to entrap him. He answers them in language never to be forgotten. Two incidents relieve the trials of the day and bring joy to the Saviour's heart: the poor widow's gift, and the visit of the Greeks. As they pass out of the temple the disciples call the Lord's attention to it, but he prophesies its destruction.

We pass out to the Mount of Olives and there hear the echo of the Lord's warning regarding the impending doom of the city and the end of the world. How real it all seems as we look westward upon the Jerusalem of to-day, a mere shadow of the former city! There were uttered those wonderful parables of the figless fig tree, the wise and foolish virgins, and the men with the talents.

Then, probably late in the evening, the company returns to Bethany, while Judas plots to betray the Lord into the hands of his enemies.

Wednesday, April 5.

A day of retirement, probably spent in Bethany.

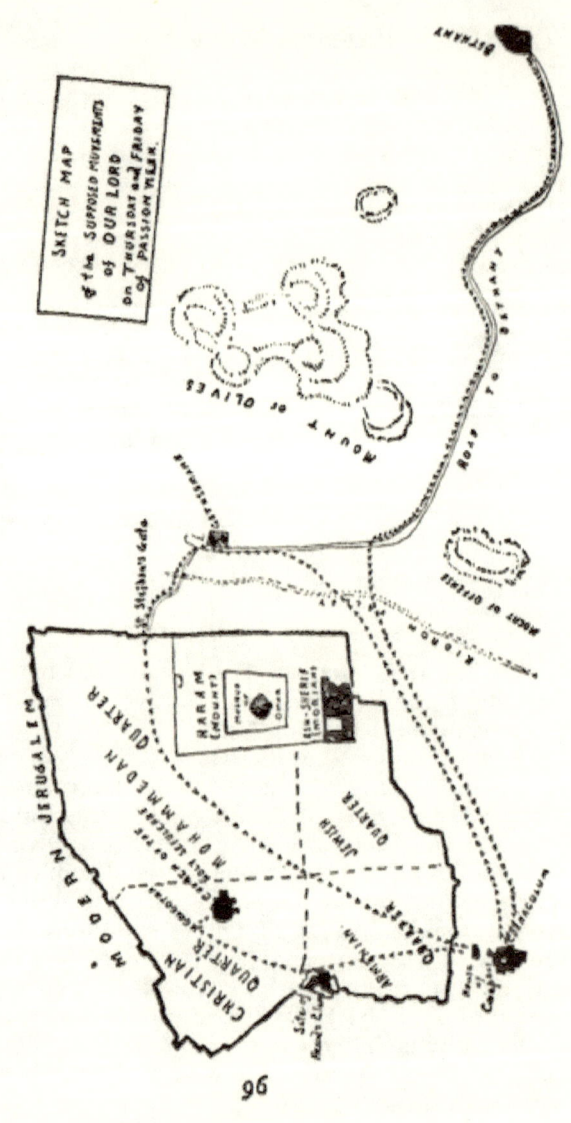

Passion Week

Thursday, April 6.

FROM BETHANY TO JERUSALEM—"UPPER ROOM"—GETHSEMANE.

Peter and John sent ahead to prepare the
    passover, ... Matt. xxvi, 17-19; Mark xiv, 12-16; Luke xxii, 7-13.
Jesus follows in the evening with the other
    disciples; joins the twelve at supper, Matt. xxvi, 20; Mark xiv, 17; Luke xxii, 14.
In the "upper room;" Strife for first place, . . . Luke xxii, 24-30.
Jesus washes his disciples' feet, ... John xiii, 1-20.
Announcement of betrayal—Judas
    goes out, . . . Matt. xxvi. 21-25; Mark xiv, 18-21; John xiii, 21-30.
The supper, . . . Matt. xxvi, 26-29; Mark xiv, 22-25; Luke xxii, 14-20.
Peter protests his faithfulness—the Lord
    warns him, ... Luke xxii, 31-38; John xiii, 36-38.
The last teaching, ... John xiv, xv, xvi.
Jesus prays, ... John xvii.
From the "upper room" to Gethsemane; On
    the way, ... Matt. xxvi, 30; John xviii, 1.
The agony in the garden, . . . Matt. xxvi, 36-46; Mark xiv, 32-42.
The arrest, Matt. xxvi, 47-56; Mark xiv, 43-52; Luke xxii, 47-53; John xviii, 2-12.

After a day of rest the Lord enters upon his final struggle with his enemies. Peter and John are sent some time during the day to prepare the passover for themselves and the others who follow toward evening. The traditional site of the "upper room," where Jesus and his disciples ate the passover, is known as the Cœnaculum, situated on Mount Zion, at the southwest corner of the present city, just outside the walls. It is a room in a Mohammedan mosque known as Neby Daud (Prophet David). It is a large and dreary room of stone, some thirty feet wide by sixty feet long, and is divided in the center by columns. The building in which the Cœnaculum is located "was formerly a Christian church, and is of very high antiquity (mentioned as early as the fourth century), and was early held to be the place where the apostles were assembled at Pentecost when the Holy Ghost descended upon them. As it is probable that they were assembled in the same place where the Lord's Supper was instituted the tradition, at least as regards the site, seems quite credible."[1] We can reach this traditional site by leaving the Bethany road after crossing the Mount of Olives and just before entering the city, and turning westward through the valley of the Kidron, skirting the southern wall. The Neby Daud, in which the Cœnaculum is situated, lies just south of the American cemetery.

The kind of table at which Jesus and the twelve sat we do

---
[1] Andrews *The Life of Our Lord.*

In His Footsteps

not know, nor do we know the order at the table. John, we are told, sat nearest the Lord, and evidently Judas was not the farthest away. Edersheim believes that the traitor "claimed and obtained the chief seat at the table next the Lord."

They had just been seated when strife breaks out among the disciples as to which should have the chief place in the Lord's kingdom. They were still clinging to the belief that Christ would establish a worldly rule, and that he would choose certain favorites for high positions. Jesus had often explained the nature of his kingdom, but now he will illustrate it. It was customary for a servant with water and towels to pass among the guests cleansing the hands and feet of each from the dust of travel. While the disciples are quarreling over who shall have the highest place and be given honorable titles, and have servants to run upon their errands, their Lord is passing from one to the other washing the feet of each. Even Judas is not passed by.

They are now ready for the supper which Peter and John had provided. It was the beginning of the great feast of the passover, which had been instituted to commemorate "the deliverance of the Jews in Egypt from the destroying angel when all the firstborn of the Egyptians were slain" (Exod. xii, 14). This remarkable deliverance was ever after to be commemorated by a feast of seven days, the feast of unleavened bread. But *distinct from this feast and introductory to it* was the paschal supper, or 'the Lord's passover.' The people being divided into households or families of not less than ten nor more than twenty persons, a lamb was slain for each family and afterward eaten with unleavened bread and bitter herbs. Now followed a feast of seven days' continuance in which the bread eaten was unleavened."[1] The supper at which Jesus and the twelve now sat was this paschal supper which introduced the seven days' feast. It was at the very beginning of the supper that the Lord said, "One of you will betray me." The separation of Judas from the company is the sign for the continuance of the meal. "Each ate and drank at his will; all alike, in the patriarchal way of the East, lifting what they wished with their fingers from the common dish. A third cup of wine passed round marked the close of the feast as a religious solemnity. He was about

---

[1] Andrews, *The Life of Our Lord.*

Passion Week

to leave them, and as yet they had no rite, however simple, to form a center round which they might permanently gather. Some emblem was needed by which they might hereafter be distinguished; some common bond, which should outwardly link them to each other and to their common Master. The passover had been the symbol of the theocracy of the past, and had given the people of God an outward ever-recurring remembrance of their relations to each other and their invisible King. As the founder of the new Israel, Jesus would now institute a special rite for its members in all ages and countries. The old covenant of God with the Jews had found its vivid embodiment in the yearly festivity he had that night for the last time observed. The new covenant must, henceforth, have an outward embodiment also; more spiritual, as became it, but equally vivid.

"Nothing could have been more touching and beautiful in its simplicity than the symbol now introduced. The third cup was known as 'the cup of blessing,' and had marked the close of the meal, held to do honor to the economy now passing away. The bread had been handed round with the words, 'This is the bread of affliction;' and the flesh of the lamb had been distributed with the words, 'This is the body of the passover.' The feast of the ancient people of God having been honored by these striking utterances, Jesus took one of the loaves or cakes before him, gave thanks, broke it, and handed it to the apostles with words, the repetition almost exactly of those they had heard a moment before, 'Take, eat'; this is my body, which is given for you: this do in remembrance of me.' Then taking the cup, which had been filled for the fourth and last handing round, he gave thanks to God once more, and passed it to the circle, with the words, 'Drink ye all of it, for this cup is the new covenant,' presently to be made 'in my blood;' instead of the covenant made also in blood by God with your fathers; 'it is' an abiding symbol, 'my blood of the covenant of my Father with the new Israel, which is shed for you for the remission of sins. This do, as often as ye drink it, in remembrance of me.'"[1]

Some time during the meal, or just at its close, Peter protests his faithfulness, followed by the Lord's warning. Then the Lord spoke those comforting words recorded by John (chapters xiv, xv, xvi), in which he compares himself to a

---

[1] Geikie, *Life of Christ*.

vine, exhorts his disciples not to be discouraged, and promises the Holy Spirit. The prayer of the Lord follows.

It is between ten and twelve o'clock, and Jesus with the eleven turns from the "upper room" toward the Mount of Olives. If the room was where tradition places it the company would probably pass through the southern edge of the city—we now skirt the southern wall on the outside—to a garden on the Mount of Olives, called the garden of Geth-

THE GARDEN OF GETHSEMANE.

semane. We descend into the valley of the Kidron, cross a bridge, and are on the traditional site of the place where the Lord experienced that awful agony and bloody sweat. The word Gethsemane signifies *oil press.* We enter the garden through a wall erected in 1847. A rock near the gate "marks the spot where Peter, James, and John slept." A fragment of a column "indicates the traditional place where Judas be-

Passion Week

trayed Jesus with a kiss." The present garden "contains eight venerable olive trees, with trunks burst from age and shored up with stones, which are said to date from the time of Christ."[1]

The officers, led by the traitor Judas, at last arrive. The Lord is revealed by a kiss. Peter nobly but with mistaken zeal defends his Master. Jesus is then put under arrest.

Friday, April 7.

FROM GETHSEMANE TO THE HOUSE OF ANNAS, THENCE TO PALACE OF CAIAPHAS, PALACE OF HEROD, GOLGOTHA, AND THE SEPULCHER.

Short stay at house of Annas, ... John xviii, 13, 14.
Peter and John follow to palace of Caiaphas,
    Matt. xxvi, 57, 58; Mark xiv, 53, 54; Luke xxii, 54, 55; John xviii, 15.
Trial of Jesus before Jewish authorities,
    Matt. xxvi, 59-68; Mark xiv, 55-65; Luke xxii, 63-71; John xviii, 19-24.
Peter's denial,
    Matt. xxvi, 69-75; Mark xiv, 66-72; Luke xxii, 56-62; John xviii, 16-18, 25-27.
From palace of Caiaphas to Pilate's judgment seat: Trial before Pilate,
    Matt. xxvii, 2, 11-31a; Mark xv, 1-20a; Luke xxiii, 1-25; John xviii, 28; xix, 16a.
From Pilate's judgment seat to Golgotha: On the way,
    Matt. xxvii, 31b, 32; Mark xv, 20b, 21; Luke xxiii, 26-32; John xix, 16b, 17.
The crucifixion: Superscription
    on the cross, Matt. xxvii, 37; Mark xv, 26; Luke xxiii, 38; John xix, 19-22.
First word from the cross, ... Luke xxiii, 33, 34.
Soldiers cast
    lots, . Matt. xxvii, 35, 36; Mark xv, 24; Luke xxiii, 34; John xix, 23, 24.
Jews mock at Jesus, Matt. xxvii, 39-44; Mark xv, 29-32; Luke xxiii, 35-37.
Second word from the cross, ... Luke xxiii, 39-43.
Third word from the cross, ... John xix, 25-27.
Darkness, ... Matt. xxvii, 45; Mark xv, 33; Luke xxiii, 44, 45.
Fourth word from the cross, . . Matt. xxvii, 46, 47; Luke xv, 34, 35.
Fifth word from the cross, Matt. xxvii, 48, 49; Mark xv, 36; John xix, 28, 29.
Sixth word from the cross, ... John xix, 30.
Seventh word, ... Luke xxiii, 46.
Jesus dies—earth-
    quake, Matt. xxvii, 50-56; Mark xv, 37-41; Luke xxiii, 45-49; John xix, 30.
Jesus pierced with a spear, ... John xix, 31-37.
From Golgotha to Joseph's tomb: The burial of Jesus,
    Matt. xxvii, 57 61; Mark xv, 42-47; Luke xxiii, 50-56; John xix, 38-42.
The watch at the sepulcher, ... Matt. xxvii, 62-66.

Some think the earliest events noted for this day, such as the trial of Jesus, etc., took place before midnight on Thursday. We cannot say. But it seems improbable that so much could be crowded into Thursday. The point of time, however, has little bearing on the events themselves.

Though Annas was not now high priest, having been deposed from office, he was the father-in-law of Caiaphas, the actual high priest, and was regarded, both on account of his relationship to Caiaphas and his long experience, with great

---

[1] Baedeker, *Palestine and Syria.*

In His Footsteps

respect by the Jewish people. We do not know where his house was, but probably it was not far from the palace of Caiaphas; indeed, the apartments of Annas and Caiaphas may have joined. Jesus is taken directly from Gethsemane to Annas, thence to Caiaphas, who examines him briefly. The traditional site of the palace or house of Caiaphas is just north of the Cœnaculum, where Jesus ate the last supper with his disciples. The Sanhedrin, or Jewish council, was at once convened, and Jesus is put on trial, condemned, and afterward reviled by the members of that body. During the trial Peter denies his Lord. At daybreak the Sanhedrin is again convened "to determine how to bring Jesus before Pilate; and at this time his confession is repeated, but without a formal trial."

The Lord is then taken to Pilate for sentence of death. As a rule the Roman courts did not open before six o'clock in the morning. It is not known whether Pilate's court was held in the fortress of Antonia, near the temple, or in the palace of Herod the Great. "We consider it most probable," says Andrews, "that all the judicial proceedings before Pilate were at the palace of Herod upon Mount Zion." It was situated on "the north side of Mount Zion, and was a magnificent building of marble, with which, according to Josephus, the temple itself bore no comparison. It is to be distinguished from the palace of Solomon, which was lower down on the side of the mount." After much discussion and many efforts to release Jesus, Pilate condemns him to death.

We can almost hear the echo of the terrible words, "Crucify! Crucify!" as we follow our Lord when he turns from Pilate's judgment seat toward Golgotha. He went forth bearing his cross, a burden of perhaps one hundred and fifty pounds in weight. The scenes through which he has just passed must have greatly weakened him, for, while there is no record that he fell, he must have showed signs of extreme prostration. The burden of the cross is put upon the shoulders of one Simon, a resident of Cyrene, in North Africa. The Lord, surrounded by a motley crowd, with no friends but the few faithful souls who follow in the distance, passes down the sorrowful way to the place of crucifixion. We try to find his footsteps after all the centuries have swept their *débris* upon them, but it is an impossible task, some of the present streets being from forty to fifty feet above those of the ancient

Passion Week

city. The site of Golgotha is not known, but it was outside the walls, probably toward the northwest.[1] "From the palace of Herod the sad procession must have passed out under the great castles of Hippicus, Phasael, and Mariamne, through the Hebron or Jaffa gate or the gate Gennath. As it moved slowly on an official proclaimed aloud the names of the prisoners and the offenses for which they were about to die."[2]

The cross had long been used by Egyptians, Greeks, and Romans, but never by the Jews. Now, however, so eager are they for Jesus's death that any means of accomplishing their purpose is accepted. The company arrived at Golgotha about 9 A.M. Jesus, with two malefactors, is at once fastened to the cross, his robe meanwhile having been taken from him. By three o'clock in the afternoon the veil of the temple is rent. The earthquake and the darkness mark the Lord's last conscious moments.

Before six o'clock the body has been reverently carried by loving hands to the sepulcher, which was near the place of execution.

Saturday, April 8.

Jesus in the tomb.

---

[1] A site on the north has been selected by Conder and others as the scene of the crucifixion, but it has nothing but conjecture in its favor.
[2] Geikie, *Life of Christ*.

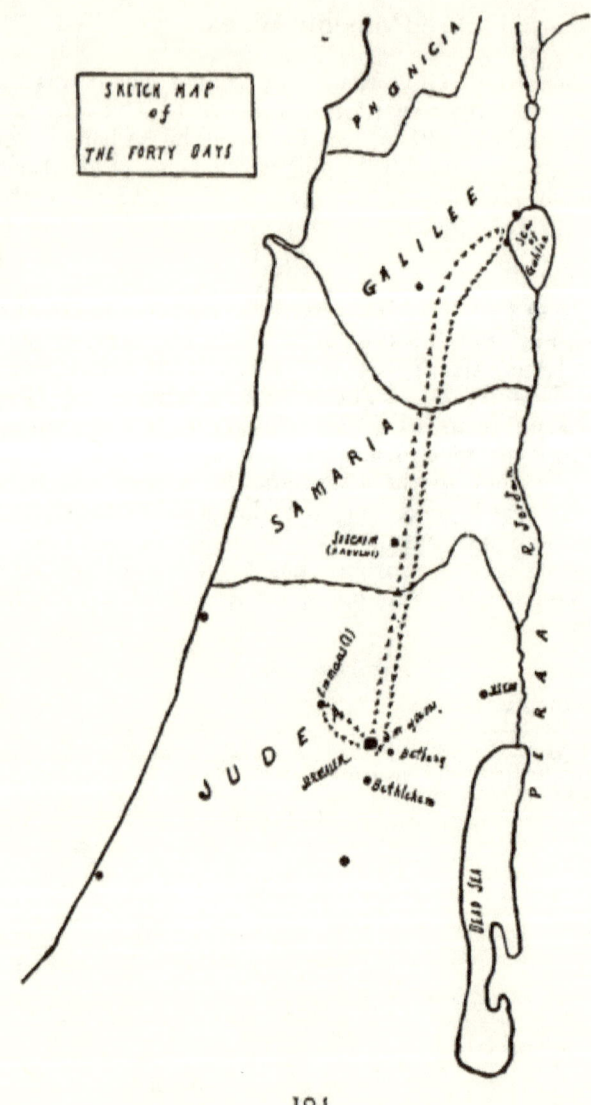

The Forty Days—Resurrection to Ascension

CHAPTER VIII.

The Forty Days, from the Resurrection to the Ascension, A. D. 30.

INTINERARY ON MAP.—Jerusalem—Emmaus—Jerusalem—Sea of Galilee—Mountain in Galilee—Mount of Olives.

IN JERUSALEM.

Sunday, April 9, Forenoon.[1]

The morning of the resurrection—an earthquake,	Matt. xxviii, 2-4.
The women come to the tomb, Matt. xxviii, 1; Mark xvi, 1-4; Luke xxiv, 1, 2;	John xx, 1.
Mary Magdalene calls Peter and John,	John xx, 2.
The women at the tomb, Matt. xxviii, 5-8; Mark xvi, 5-8;	Luke xxiv, 3-8.
Peter and John at the tomb,	Luke xxiv, 12; John xx, 3-10.
The Lord appears to Mary Magdalene,	Mark xvi, 9-11; John xx, 11-18.
He appears to the women,	Matt. xxviii, 9, 10; Luke xxiv, 9-11.
The guard report to the priests,	Matt. xxviii, 11-15.

TO those faithful ones who had with much misgiving and many doubts, yet with constantly increasing love, followed Jesus day by day during his ministry and through the sorrowful week of his passion, and at last to the cross, his death must have seemed like an insurmountable wall or fathomless chasm across the path of the traveler. They knew not where to turn. Their leader was dead, and there seemed nothing in life for them. Had this been the end we should not be in Palestine to-day trying to mark the footsteps of Jesus. We have, it is true, gone to his grave with heavy hearts on account of his great sufferings, yet with a secret joy, for we know what the early followers of his footsteps did not know, that the grave cannot hold the Lord. He must rise again to live forever our glorified Redeemer.

It is Sunday morning—Easter Sunday. There has been an earthquake. An angel has rolled away the stone from the door of the tomb. Mary Magdalene and the other women from Galilee come with sweet spices to anoint the Lord's

---

[1] The following harmony is from Andrews, *The Life of Our Lord.*

body. They see the stone rolled away, and Mary Magdalene, believing that the enemies of Christ had stolen his body, hurries away to tell Peter and John. The other women pass on to the sepulcher and meet an angel, who tells them that the Lord has risen and will meet the disciples in Galilee. Peter and John then come running, followed by Mary Mag-

ROCK TOMB WITH ROLLING STONE DOOR.

dalene. The two men enter the sepulcher, finding nothing within but the graveclothes. They leave the tomb, but Mary remains weeping. Looking into the sepulcher she sees two angels, and shortly afterward Jesus himself appears and speaks to her, giving her a message for the disciples. After that the

The Forty Days—Resurrection to Ascension

Lord appears to the two women who had been to the city, and who were accompanied by others, and permits them to worship him.

The question of the location of the sepulcher is involved in that regarding the site of the crucifixion. Tradition points to the spot already named, just outside the walls (the ancient, not the present walls) on the northwest. Bishop Eusebius, born about the middle of the third century after Christ, says that during the excavations made in the reign of Constantine the tomb of Christ was discovered. There is an old and fanciful tale to the effect that Helena, Constantine's mother, by the aid of a miracle, found not only the Lord's sepulcher, but also his cross. Here a church was built and consecrated in the year 336. The present edifice, known as the "Church of the Sepulcher," was built by Greek and Armenian Christians in 1810. Childish credulity or deliberate fraud,

THE CHURCH OF THE HOLY SEPULCHER, JERUSALEM

probably a mixture of both, has located everything connected with the crucifixion and entombment. Even the "Hole of the Cross" is identified. During the Easter festival the church is "crowded with pilgrims of every nationality," and there is usually a disgraceful riot between the different sects, which requires all the force of the Mohammedan police to quell. A most disgraceful spectacle is the

In His Footsteps

so-called miracle of the Holy Fire, managed by the Greeks. Of course, it is an out-and-out fraud. "On Easter Eve, about 2 P. M., a procession of the superior clergy moves round the sepulcher, all lamps having been carefully extinguished in view of the crowd. Some members of the higher order of the priesthood enter the chapel of the sepulcher, while the priests pray and the people are in the utmost suspense. At

PILGRIM IN THE CHURCH OF THE HOLY SEPULCHER.

length the fire, which has come down from heaven (as the priests say), is pushed through a window of the sepulcher, and there now follows an indescribable tumult, everyone endeavoring to be the first to get his taper lighted. In a few moments the whole church is illuminated."[1] In 1834, when more than six thousand persons were in the church, there was a riot at this ceremony, and about three hundred were killed.

---

[1] Baedeker: *Palestine and Syria.*

The Forty Days—Resurrection to Ascension

FROM JERUSALEM TO EMMAUS—RETURN TO JERUSALEM.

Sunday, April 9, Afternoon.

Jesus appears to two disciples on
  the way to Emmaus, . . . Mark xvi, 12, 13; Luke xxiv, 13-32.
Appears to all the apostles in
  Jerusalem, except Thomas, Mark xvi, 14; Luke xxiv, 32-48; John xx, 19-23.

Sunday, April 16.

Appears to all the apostles, ... John xx, 26-29.

Some time during the latter part of Easter Sunday the Lord joins two of his disciples as they journey to a village called Emmaus, distant from Jerusalem sixty furlongs (seven and one half miles). There are at least four places which are named by modern scholars as the Emmaus of Christ's time. The best evidence seems to lie with a village now known as El Kubebeh, northwest of Jerusalem. We find there a Franciscan monastery, built in 1862, which "is said to stand on the spot where Jesus brake bread with the two disciples."

The two disciples return at once to the city and join the rest of the eleven. "The place where the apostles were assembled was, in all probability, the same in which they had eaten the paschal supper, and to which they returned from the Mount of Olives after the Ascension."[1]

A week later, probably in the same place, Thomas being present, the Lord again appears. He shows the print of the nails and of the spear.

FROM JERUSALEM TO THE SEA OF GALILEE.

Reappears to the seven disciples in Galilee, . John xxi, 1-3.
Miracle of the fishes, ... John xxi, 4-11.
At a meal Jesus counsels Peter, . . . John xxi, 12-23.

A part of the disciples have returned to the old haunts beside the Sea of Galilee—back to their nets, as though there were no world to be evangelized. There Jesus comes, works a miracle, and joins them at a simple meal. His counsel to Peter is very tender, but very searching. "Feed my sheep; feed my lambs," we hear him say. Those last words, "Follow thou me," suggest a life-long pilgrimage, not merely marking his earthly footsteps, but imitating his life.

---

[1] Andrews.

In His Footsteps

FROM THE SEA OF GALILEE TO A MOUNTAIN IN GALILEE.
Appears to the disciples; the "Great Commission," . . . . . Matt. xxviii, 16-20; Mark xvi 15-18.

What mountain it was where the Lord met his disciples for the last time in Galilee we do not know. There he gave his great commission to go into all the world, making disciples of all nations.

FROM A MOUNTAIN IN GALILEE TO THE MOUNT OF OLIVES.
Last words and ascension, . . . Mark xvi, 19, 20; Luke xxiv, 44-53.

We return for the last time toward Jerusalem with our Lord. In full view of the city which so cruelly rejected him the

THE MOUNT OF OLIVES.

Lord will ascend to the right hand of the Father. It has not been an easy task to mark the footsteps of the Lord during his earthly life; but, if not easy, it has repaid us a thousandfold for every effort. Words, acts, even the silences of Christ, have taken on a new meaning as we have sought to realize the time and place of their occurrence. Above all have we been impressed with the truth of the saying of the apostle who referred to the Lord as " Jesus of Nazareth, who *went about doing good.*" How faithfully he " went about " only they can realize who try to walk where he walked.

The Lord has led out his disciples to the Mount of Olives. There is a spot marked as the scene of the ascension, but

The Forty Days—Resurrection to Ascension

there is nothing to show in its favor. St. Luke tells us that "he led them out until they were over against Bethany" (Revised Version). That would seem to show that they went eastward on the Mount of Olives until they could see Bethany in the distance. There, after a few words regarding their great work, he reminds them of the promise of the Comforter. And then "he lifted up his hands, and blessed them. And it came to pass, while he blessed them, he was parted from them, and carried up into heaven."

There we would stand gazing up into heaven, hoping to get a vision of our glorified Saviour. A peculiar loneliness steals over us. We seem like orphans, for he has gone where we can follow him no longer as the man of Nazareth. But we seem to hear his voice saying: "Let not your heart be troubled. . . . In my Father's house are many mansions: . . . I go to prepare a place for you. . . . I will come again, and receive you unto myself." We may still follow him. Heaven is our goal. The pilgrimage may not be easy, but he has gone before. Not as during his earthly life need we be uncertain of his footsteps, for he himself will be our guide "even unto the end of the world."[1]

---
[1] The return home may take the same route as that by which we came. Some may prefer to conduct the party overland through Europe, stopping at the most interesting points.

THE END.

www.ingramcontent.com/pod-product-compliance
Lightning Source LLC
Chambersburg PA
CBHW022146160426
43197CB00009B/1451